TREES BE COMPANY

TREES BE COMPANY

An Anthology of Poetry

edited by Angela King and Susan Clifford for
Common Ground

CHELSEA GREEN PUBLISHING COMPANY
White River Junction, Vermont

First published in the USA in 2001
by Chelsea Green Publishing Company
Post Office Box 428
White River Junction, Vermont 05001

All poems contained in this anthology
are copyrighted by their authors
and may not be reproduced without permission

This selection © Angela King and Sue Clifford,
Common Ground, 2001. All rights reserved.

Foreword © John Fowles 1989, 2001

Pages 191 to 205 are an extension to this copyright page.

Cover design by Rick Lawrence
Cover illustration © Clifford Harper 2001

Typeset in Sabon by Green Books, Totnes, Devon, UK

Text printed by Biddles Ltd, Guildford, Surrey
on Five Seasons 100% recycled paper

Library of Congress Cataloging-in-Publication data
available on request

ISBN 1-890132-83-7

Contents

Preface

Poetry is rich in reference to trees and woods and the spirits that we give them. In our own deciduous world, they call the seasons; they live longer and grow bigger than any other creature; they provide feasts for metaphor, symbol and allegory, and they allude to secrets of common culture long trapped in their annual rings.

Common Ground offers cultural arguments about trees and woods alongside the scientific, economic, ecological and spiritual ones sparely demonstrated in William Heyen's poem:

Emancipation Proclamation

Whereas it minds its own business
& lives in its one place so faithfully
& its trunk supports us when we lean against it
& its branches remind us of how we think

Whereas it keeps no bank account but hoards carbon
& does not discriminate between starlings and robins
& provides free housing for insects & squirrels
& lifts its heartwood grave into the air

Whereas it holds our firmament in place
& writes underground gospel with its roots
& whispers us oxygen with its leaves
& may not survive its new climate of ultraviolet

We the people for ourselves & our children
necessarily proclaim this tree
free from commerce & belonging to itself
as long as it & we shall live.

This book presents evidence of our deep cultural need for trees and woods. Our hope is that it will inspire people to take more care of them.

Trees, and indeed woods, know no distinction between town and country: they are close to everyone. But ironically, concern for loss of rainforest or rising global temperatures (the greenhouse effect) rarely brings us to care more deeply for the trees in our own street, garden or locality.

'A culture is no better than its woods', as W. H. Auden reminds us. If we are to combat local pollution, make even the slightest impact on global warming, enjoy our surroundings and share them with many other creatures, we need trees: trees here and trees now. If we are to nourish more than our prosaic needs we need their longevity, their beauty, their generosity. We are tied to the global turn of events not simply through the ecosystem, but by a universal and deeper need for trees with roots in many cultures. Trees stand for nature and culture. We shall stand or fall with them.

There are so many poems which demonstrate our imaginative relationship with trees, our selection has been guided by a desire to show that the 20th century is as rich as earlier times and we feel strongly that the contemporary poet's voice should be heard alongside that of the politician and professional environ-mentalist. We have tried to offer a variety of poets and preoccupations, sometimes sacrificing favourites on the way. Arranging the poems alphabetically by title encourages chance connections. So many poets have found richness in the theme—we had to restrict our selection to poems written in English (with a few exceptions of Welsh, Old English, Irish and Latin). One day perhaps we shall embark on the rest of the world. . . .

We have uncovered poets immersed in nature and also those who would shun such affiliations. We have found mythology and legend, languages of longevity and seasonal revolution, popular politics and the power of places, lost childhood and golden ages gone, prognoses of good or evil, misplaced love, refuge from the world's ills or one's own afflictions, solace and fears, threat and discovery, and—most frequently—a lifting of the soul: all evidence is that if we talk to the trees, they speak back to us.

Susan Clifford and Angela King
www.commonground.org.uk
February 2001

Foreword

Snottygogs. . . . this odd dialect word, so uncouth-sounding for something so pretty, somehow lodged in my mind, perhaps for its sheer inappropriateness, from the moment I first heard it. According to Geoffrey Grigson in *The Englishman's Flora*—a poem of a book, though in prose—it comes in this form from Sussex. And what are snottygogs? They are those little carmine-pink berries that festoon the dark green branches of yew, and that attract birds in early winter as ripe cherries do summer children. Yew seeds are poisonous, so are the leaves, but not the coral flesh of the little snottygogs. I have several yews, always busy with tits and goldcrests, in my Dorset garden. One of my favourite trees, its dark 'graveyard' reputation in English folklore (and poetry) is absurd and to my mind convincing proof that the closest mammal to man is not a primate, but the sheep. Only flock-belief, or total swallowing of convention, can explain the profound gloom with which we surround such a charmingly lively and sturdy tree. I suppose it is that since it can, if we are very stupid, harm us, it must therefore be very evil—an infantile logic that informs far too much of our attitude to nature.

According to a recent Greenpeace publication, *Tree Survey of Southern Britain*, yew are doing particularly badly in Dorset; nearly nine out of ten are damaged by various forms of pollution. As soon as I had read the report I rushed out to look at my own. There was a particularly rich crop of snottygogs this last year, and the old trees, such marvellous re-shooters when pruned (one reason I love them), seemed greenly flourishing. As so often these days, the reality of nature outside flagrantly contradicts the doom one reads indoors. Science is crying wolf, it seems, with none yet in sight. Would it were so, but it is not. 1989 began with a formidable warning about our endangered earth from what seemed an unlikely source: *Time* magazine. To what extent we humans are on the brink—a decade, fifty years, a century away—is a matter of dispute; but not that the nemesis is near in any real time scale.

We all know that things are very bad for trees, indeed for all nature, and all over the world; which makes writing of their plight, or making anyone listen to it, near impossible. In 'The Dream of the Rood', one of the earlier poems in this anthology, it is made a glory of the tree that it constituted the Cross and so bore the body of Christ. But it is not Christ who is crucified now; it is the tree itself, and on the bitter gallows of human greed and stupidity. Only suicidal morons, in a world already choking to death, would destroy the best natural air-conditioner creation affords; as well cut our children's throats.

We are all heir to two conflicting souls, or psyches, when it comes to nature: a green one and a black. The first, best symbolized by the tree, still retains, despite the present Gadarene influx into our nature-barren cities, at least a memory of what it was to live in balance of a kind with nature, on a green planet. The black soul, which has gained such huge power during these last two centuries, was bred by that disastrously arrogant aspect of Christianity (and other male-dominated religions) which supposed man to be in God's image and duly appointed him, like some hopelessly venal and ultimately crazed gamekeeper, the steward of all creation. Given the proliferating and savagely parasitical species mankind is, that was to place our destiny in the power of the rat, the locust, the plague. The black soul in us both fears and hates nature, and it still drives the majority.

Science, I suspect, helps rather less than we like to suppose or might wish. However well intended, or cogently presented, it tends to anaesthetize. The scientists are the experts, they must know best; I don't. Is not all the power, the knowledge of means, the authority, theirs? I need do nothing, for the very simple reason that I cannot. Science stifles instinctive feeling, and when such feeling concerns nature, it can slip with ominous ease into mere sentimentality. One might dismiss the scientific content of all the poetry here as non-existent; and so conclude that it cannot be serious or worth attention. But such smug dismissal, so typical of our science-tyrannized world, quite simply threatens to end all life on it.

The poems in this anthology remind me very much of the countless fallen leaves that litter the pavements in this time and place where I happen to write: Primrose Hill in London, December. I watch people kick rather crossly through, or fastidiously sidestep, the dead leaves; indeed treat them as most of us treat the detritus of past human feelings, which is what such collections as this represent. Messy and irritating dead leaf, so many blemishes on a supposedly proper modern world. An elderly aunt once told me a long time ago, when I was a little boy in her charge, that dead leaves were human faces. One did not tread carelessly on them, or kick them thoughtlessly aside, as I was wont.

This is how I hope this anthology will be read; whatever the poems' individual value, they are a reminder of what that city-asphyxiated green soul in all of us both was and is. To flick through them without thinking or caring is to kick through human faces, or the minds behind them. Dead leaves, whether literal or on paper, constitute the humus from which all new leaf must grow. In poetry as in life, trees are like humans: they need their pasts to feed their presents.

Destroy either, and you lose all. The black soul will have won, and the last tree died; no leaves to kick through, nor even a small boy left to kick.

John Fowles
1989

Afforestation

It's a population of trees
Colonising the old
Haunts of men; I prefer,
Listening to their talk,
The bare language of grass
To what the woods say,
Standing in black crowds
Under the stars at night
Or in the sun's way.
The grass feeds the sheep;
The sheep give the wool
For warm clothing, but these—?
I see the cheap times
Against which they grow:
Thin houses for dupes,
Pages of pale trash,
A world that has gone sour
With spruce. Cut them down,
They won't take the weight
Of any of the strong bodies
For which the wind sighs.

R. S. Thomas

Afternoon Tea

Please you, excuse me, good five-o'clock people,
    I've lost my last hatful of words,
And my heart's in the wood up above the church steeple,
    I'd rather have tea with the birds.

Gay Kate's stolen kisses, poor Barnaby's scars,
    John's losses and Mary's gains,
Oh! what do they matter, my dears, to the stars
    Or the glow-worms in the lanes!

I'd rather lie under the tall elm-trees,
    With old rooks talking loud overhead,
To watch a red squirrel run over my knees,
    Very still on my brackeny bed.

And wonder what feathers the wrens will be taking
    For lining their nests next Spring;
Or why the tossed shadow of boughs in a great wind shaking
    Is such a lovely thing.

Charlotte Mew

Alcaic

Out in the deep wood, silence and darkness fall,
down through the wet leaves comes the October mist;
    no sound, but only a blackbird scolding,
        making the mist and the darkness listen.

Peter Levi

The Almond Trees

There's nothing here
this early;
cold sand
cold churning ocean, the Atlantic,
no visible history,

except this stand
of twisted, coppery, sea-almond trees
their shining postures surely
bent as metal, and one

foam-haired, salt-grizzled fisherman,
his mongrel growling, whirling on the stick
he pitches him; its spinning rays
'no visible history'
until their lengthened shapes amaze the sun.

By noon,
this further shore of Africa is strewn
with the forked limbs of girls toasting their flesh
in scarves, sunglasses, Pompeian bikinis,

brown daphnes, laurels, they'll all have
like their originals, their sacred grove,
this frieze
of twisted, coppery, sea-almond trees.

The fierce acetylene air
has singed
their writhing trunks with rust, the same
hues as a foundered, peeling barge.
It'll sear a pale skin copper with its flame.

The sand's white-hot ash underheel,
but their aged limbs have got their brazen sheen
from fire. Their bodies fiercely shine!
They're cured,
they endured their furnace.

Aged trees and oiled limbs share a common colour!

Welded in one flame,
huddling naked, stripped of their name,
for Greek or Roman tags, they were lashed
raw by wind, washed
out with salt and fire-dried,
bitterly nourished where their branches died,

their leaves' broad dialect a coarse,
enduring sound
they shared together.

Not as some running hamadryad's cries
rooted, broke slowly into leaf
her nipples peaking to smooth, wooden boles

Their grief
howls seaward through charred, ravaged holes.

One sunburnt body now acknowledges
that past and its own metamorphosis
as, moving from the sun, she kneels to spread
her wrap within the bent arms of this grove
that grieves in silence, like parental love.

Derek Walcott

Alone in the Woods

Alone in the woods I felt
The bitter hostility of the sky and the trees
Nature has taught her creatures to hate
Man that fusses and fumes
Unquiet man
As the sap rises in the trees
As the sap paints the trees a violent green
So rises the wrath of Nature's creatures
At man
So paints the face of Nature a violent green.
Nature is sick at man
Sick at his fuss and fume
Sick at his agonies
Sick at his gaudy mind

That drives his body
Ever more quickly
More and more
In the wrong direction.

Stevie Smith

Amphion

My father left a park to me,
  But it is wild and barren,
A garden too with scarce a tree,
  And waster than a warren:
Yet say the neighbours when they call,
  It is not bad but good land,
And in it is the germ of all
  That grows within the woodland.

O had I lived when song was great
  In days of old Amphion,
And ta'en my fiddle to the gate,
  Nor cared for seed or scion!
And had I lived when song was great,
  And legs of trees were limber,
And ta'en my fiddle to the gate,
  And fiddled in the timber!

'Tis said he had a tuneful tongue,
  Such happy intonation,
Wherever he sat down and sung
  He left a small plantation;
Wherever in a lonely grove
  He set up his forlorn pipes,
The gouty oak began to move,
  And flounder into hornpipes.

The mountain stirred its bushy crown,
	And, as tradition teaches,
Young ashes pirouetted down
	Coquetting with young beeches;
And briony-vine and ivy-wreath
	Ran forward to his rhyming,
And from the valleys underneath
	Came little copses climbing.

The linden broke her ranks and rent
	The woodbine wreaths that bind her,
And down the middle, buzz! she went
	With all her bees behind her;
The poplars, in long order due,
	With cypress promenaded,
The shock-head willows two and two
	By rivers gallopaded.

Came wet-shod alder from the wave,
	Came yews, a dismal coterie;
Each plucked his one foot from the grave,
	Poussetting with a sloe-tree:
Old elms came breaking from the vine,
	The vine streamed out to follow,
And, sweating rosin, plumped the pine
	From many a cloudy hollow.

And wasn't it a sight to see,
	When, ere his song was ended,
Like some great landslip, tree by tree,
	The country-side descended;
And shepherds from the mountain-eaves
	Looked down, half-pleased, half-frightened,
As dashed about the drunken leaves
	The random sunshine lightened!

Oh, nature first was fresh to men,
	And wanton without measure;

So youthful and so flexile then,
      You moved her at your pleasure.
Twang out, my fiddle! shake the twigs!
      And make her dance attendance;
Blow, flute, and stir the stiff-set sprigs,
      And scirrhous roots and tendons.

'Tis vain! in such a brassy age
      I could not move a thistle;
The very sparrows in the hedge
      Scarce answer to my whistle;
Or at the most, when three-parts-sick
      With strumming and with scraping,
A jackass heehaws from the rick,
      The passive oxen gaping.

But what is that I hear? a sound
      Like sleepy counsel pleading;
O Lord! –'tis in my neighbour's ground,
      The modern Muses reading.
They read Botanic Treatises,
      And Works on Gardening through there,
And Methods of transplanting trees
      To look as if they grew there.

The withered Misses! how they prose
      O'er books of travelled seamen,
And show you slips of all that grows
      From England to Van Diemen.
They read in arbours clipt and cut,
      And alleys, faded places,
By squares of tropic summer shut
      And warmed in crystal cases.

But these, though fed with careful dirt,
      Are neither green nor sappy;
Half-conscious of the garden-squirt,
      The spindlings look unhappy.

Better to me the meanest weed
    That blows upon its mountain,
The vilest herb that runs to seed
    Beside its native fountain.

And I must work through months of toil,
    And years of cultivation,
Upon my proper patch of soil
    To grow my own plantation.
I'll take the showers as they fall,
    I will not vex my bosom:
Enough if at the end of all
    A little garden blossom.

Alfred, Lord Tennyson

Apple Poem

Take the apple from the bowl or bough
Or kitchen table where in gloom it glows
And you will sense, mysteriously, how
Its fragrant and substantial presence throws
A shadow shape of this one's red and green.
Whatever it may be—Rose of Bern,
Spice Pippin, Golden Russet, Hawthorn Dean—
Across the mind and then you may discern
Through every sense the quintessential fruit,
Perfected properties all apples own,
In this platonic shadow; absolute
This pleasing thing that you alone have grown.

Beneath the apple's skin, its green or gold,
Yellow, red or streaked with varied tints,
The white flesh tempts, sharp or sweet, quite cold.
Its blood is colourless; scent teases, hints

At othernesses that you can't define;
The taste of innocence, so slow to fade,
Persists like memory. This fruit is wine
And bread; is eucharistic. It has played
Its role in epics, fairy-tales, among
Most races of the earth; made prophecies
Of marriages and kept the Norse Gods young;
Shone like moons on Hesperidian trees.

And here, domestic, familiar as a pet,
Plump as your granny's cheek, prepared to be
Translated into jam or jelly, yet
It still retains a curious mystery.
Forget the holy leaves, the pagan lore,
And that you munch on legends when you eat,
But see, as you crunch closer to the core,
Those little pips, diminutive and neat
Containers aping tiny beetles or
Microscopic purses, little beads,
Each holding in its patient dark a store
Of apples, flowering orchards, countless seeds.

Vernon Scannell

'Autumn again, you wouldn't know in the city'

. . . Autumn again, you wouldn't know in the city
Gotta come out in a car see the birds
   flock by the yellow bush—
In Autumn, in autumn, this part of the planet's
   famous for red leaves—
Difficult for Man on earth to 'scape the snares of delusion—
 All wrong, the thought process screamed at
      from Infancy,
The Self built with myriad thoughts
  from football to I Am That I Am,

Difficult to stop breathing factory smoke,
Difficult to step out of clothes,
        hard to forget the green parka—
Trees scream & drop
            bright Leaves,
Yea Trees scream & drop bright leaves,
Difficult to get out of bed in the morning
                in the slums—
Even sex happiness a long drawn-out scheme
        To keep the mind moving—

Big gray truck rolling down highway
        to unload wares—
Bony white branches of birch relieved of their burden
—overpass, overpass, overpass
        crossing the road, more traffic
            between the cities,
                More sex carried near and far—
            Blinking tail lights
        To the Veterans hospital where we can all collapse,
Forget Pleasure and Ambition,
        be tranquil and let leaves
            blush, turned on
by the lightningbolt doctrine that rings
                        telephones
        interrupting my pleasurable humiliating dream
            in the locker room
                    last nite?—
Weeping Willow, what's your catastrophe?
    Red Red oak, oh, what's your worry? . . .

Allen Ginsberg
from Autumn Gold: New England Fall

A Barbican Ash

City pigeons on the air
planing like surfers swirl in their
calm descent, skid on one wing
about a tree where no sapling
was yesterday. Their country cousins,
counties away, now circle in
search of a nest not to be found
between the holed sky and the holed ground.
Like a flag at its masthead frayed
with shot, in this I read
of a tree winched from a wood
to be set in a concrete glade.
Workmen today come packing
its roots with a chemical Spring.

Men are more mobile than trees:
but have, when transplanted to cities,
no mineral extract of manure,
hormone or vitamin to ensure
that their roots survive, carve through the stone
roots, cable roots, strangling my own.

Jon Stallworthy

Bare Almond-Trees

Wet almond-trees, in the rain,
Like iron sticking grimly out of earth;
Black almond trunks, in the rain,
Like iron implements twisted, hideous, out of the earth,
Out of the deep, soft fledge of Sicilian winter-green,
Earth-grass uneatable,
Almond trunks curving blackly, iron-dark, climbing the slopes.

Almond-tree, beneath the terrace rail,
Black, rusted, iron trunk,
You have welded your thin stems finer,
Like steel, like sensitive steel in the air,
Grey, lavender, sensitive steel, curving thinly and brittly
    up in a parabola.

What are you doing in the December rain?
Have you a strange electric sensitiveness in your steel tips?
Do you feel the air for electric influences
Like some strange magnetic apparatus?
Do you take in messages, in some strange code,
From heaven's wolfish, wandering electricity, that prowls
    so constantly round Etna?
Do you take the whisper of sulphur from the air?
Do you hear the chemical accents of the sun?
Do you telephone the roar of the waters over the earth?
And from all this, do you make calculations?

Sicily, December's Sicily in a mass of rain
With iron branching blackly, rusted like old, twisted
        implements
And brandishing and stooping over earth's wintry fledge,
    climbing the slopes
Of uneatable soft green!

Taormina.

D. H. Lawrence

The Battle of the Trees

The tops of the beech tree
Have sprouted of late,
Are changed and renewed
From their withered state.

When the beech prospers,
Though spells and litanies
The oak tops entangle,
There is hope for trees.

I have plundered the fern,
  Through all secrets I spy,
Old Math ap Mathonwy
  Knew no more than I.

With nine sorts of faculty
  God had gifted me:
I am fruits of fruits gathered
  From nine sorts of tree—

Plum, quince, whortle, mulberry,
  Raspberry, pear,
Black cherry and white
  With the sorb in me share.

From my seat at Fefynedd,
  A city that is strong,
I watched the trees and green things
  Hastening along.

Retreating from happiness
  They would fain be set
In forms of the chief letters
  Of the alphabet.

Wayfarers wondered,
  Warriors were dismayed
At renewal of conflicts
  Such as Gwydion made,

At a battle raging
  Under each tongue root
Of a hundred-headed thing,
  A monstrous brute,

A toad with a hundred claws
  Armed at his thighs;
And in his head-recesses
  Raging likewise.

The alders in the front line
  Began the affray.
Willow and rowan-tree
  Were tardy in array.

The holly, dark green,
  Made a resolute stand;
He is armed with many spear points
  Wounding the hand.

With foot-beat of the swift oak
  Heaven and earth rung;
'Stout Guardian of the Door,'
  His name in every tongue.

Great was the gorse in battle,
  And the ivy at his prime;
The hazel was arbiter
  At this charmed time.

Uncouth and savage was the fir,
  Cruel the ash-tree—
Turns not aside a foot-breadth,
  Straight at the heart runs he.

The birch, though very noble,
  Armed himself but late:
A sign not of cowardice
  But of high estate.

The heath gave consolation
  To the toil-spent folk,
The long-enduring poplars
  In battle much broke.

Some of them were cast away
    On the field of fight
Because of holes torn in them
    By the enemy's might.

Very wrathful was the vine
    Whose henchmen are the elms;
I exalt him mightily
    To rulers of realms.

Strong chieftains were the blackthorn
    With his ill fruit,
The unbeloved whitethorn
    Who wears the same suit,

The swift-pursuing reed
    The broom with his brood,
And the furze but ill-behaved
    Until he is subdued.

The dower-scattering yew
    Stood glum at the fight's fringe,
With the elder slow to burn
    Amid fires that singe,

And the blessed wild apple
    Laughing in pride
From the *Gorchan* of Maelderw
    By the rock side.

In shelter linger
    Privet and woodbine,
Inexperienced in warfare,
    And the courtly pine.

But I, although slighted
  Because I was not big,
Fought, trees, in your array
  On the field of Goddeu Brig.

Robert Graves

'Bear me, Pomona! to thy citron groves'

. . .Bear me, Pomona! to thy citron groves;
To where the lemon and the piercing lime,
With the deep orange glowing through the green,
Their lighter glories blend. Lay me reclined
Beneath the spreading tamarind, that shakes,
Fanned by the breeze, its fever-cooling fruit.
Deep in the night the massy locust sheds
Quench my hot limbs; or lead me through the maze,
Embowering endless, of the Indian fig;
Or, thrown at gayer ease on some fair brow,
Let me behold, by breezy murmurs cooled,
Broad o'er my head the verdant cedar wave,
And high palmettos lift their graceful shade.
Oh, stretched amid these orchards of the sun,
Give me to drain the cocoa's milky bowl,
And from the palm to draw its freshening wine!
More bounteous far than all the frantic juice
Which Bacchus pours. Nor, on its slender twigs
Low-bending, be the full pomegranate scorned;
Nor, creeping through the woods, the gelid race
Of berries. Oft in humble station dwells
Unboastful worth, above fastidious pomp.

Witness, thou best Anana, thou the pride
Of vegetable life, beyond whate'er
The poet's imaged in the golden age:
Quick let me strip thee of thy tufty coat,
Spread thy ambrosial stores, and feast with Jove!. . .

James Thomson
from The Seasons: Summer

Beech

They will not go. These leaves insist on staying.
Coinage like theirs looked frail six weeks ago.
What hintings at, excitement of delaying,
Almost as if some richer fruits could grow

If leaves hung on against each swipe of storm,
If branches bent but still did not give way.
Today is brushed with sun. The leaves are warm.
I picked one from the pavement and it lay

With borrowed shining on my Winter hand.
Persistence of this nature sends the pulse
Beating more rapidly. When will it end,

That pride of leaves? When will the branches be
Utterly bare, and seem like something else,
Now half-forgotten, no part of a tree?

Elizabeth Jennings

Beech Tree

I planted in February
A bronze-leafed beech,
In the chill brown soil
I spread out its silken fibres.

Protected it from the goats
With wire netting
And fixed it firm against
The worrying wind.

Now it is safe, I said,
April must stir
My precious baby
To greenful loveliness.

It is August now, I have hoped
But I hope no more—
My beech tree will never hide sparrows
From hungry hawks.

Patrick Kavanagh

Binsey Poplars
felled 1879

My aspens dear, whose airy cages quelled,
Quelled or quenched in leaves the leaping sun,
All felled, felled, are all felled;
   Of a fresh and following folded rank
      Not spared, not one
      That dandled a sandalled
    Shadow that swam or sank
On meadow and river and wind-wandering weed-
   winding bank.

O if we but knew what we do
        When we delve or hew—
Hack and rack the growing green!
        Since country is so tender
        To touch, her being so slender,
        That, like this sleek and seeing ball
        But a prick will make no eye at all,
        Where we, even where we mean

        To mend her we end her,
        When we hew or delve:
After-comers cannot guess the beauty been.
        Ten or twelve, only ten or twelve
        Strokes of havoc unselve
        The sweet especial scene,
        Rural scene, a rural scene,
        Sweet especial rural scene.

Gerard Manley Hopkins

Birches

When I see birches bend to left and right
Across the lines of straighter darker trees,
I like to think some boy's been swinging them.
But swinging doesn't bend them down to stay
As ice-storms do. Often you must have seen them
Loaded with ice a sunny winter morning
After a rain. They click upon themselves
As the breeze rises, and turn many-colored
As the stir cracks and crazes their enamel.
Soon the sun's warmth makes them shed crystal shells
Shattering and avalanching on the snow-crust—
Such heaps of broken glass to sweep away
You'd think the inner dome of heaven had fallen.

They are dragged to the withered bracken by the load,
And they seem not to break; though once they are bowed
So low for long, they never right themselves:
You may see their trunks arching in the woods
Years afterwards, trailing their leaves on the ground
Like girls on hands and knees that throw their hair
Before them over their heads to dry in the sun.
But I was going to say when Truth broke in
With all her matter-of-fact about the ice-storm
I should prefer to have some boy bend them
As he went out and in to fetch the cows—
Some boy too far from town to learn baseball,
Whose only play was what he found himself,
Summer or winter, and could play alone.
One by one he subdued his father's trees
By riding them down over and over again
Until he took the stiffness out of them,
And not one but hung limp, not one was left
For him to conquer. He learned all there was
To learn about not launching out too soon
And so not carrying the tree away
Clear to the ground. He always kept his poise
To the top branches, climbing carefully
With the same pains you use to fill a cup
Up to the brim, and even above the brim.
Then he flung outward, feet first, with a swish,
Kicking his way down through the air to the ground.
So was I once myself a swinger of birches.
And so I dream of going back to be.
It's when I'm weary of considerations,
And life is too much like a pathless wood
Where your face burns and tickles with the cobwebs
Broken across it, and one eye is weeping
From a twig's having lashed across it open.
I'd like to get away from earth a while
And then come back to it and begin over.

May no fate willfully misunderstand me
And half grant what I wish and snatch me away
Not to return. Earth's the right place for love:
I don't know where it's likely to go better.
I'd like to go by climbing a birch tree,
And climb black branches up a snow-white trunk
Toward heaven, till the tree could bear no more,
But dipped its top and set me down again.
That would be good both going and coming back.
One could do worse than be a swinger of birches.

Robert Frost

Blunden's Beech

I named it Blunden's Beech; and no one knew
That this—of local beeches—was the best.
Remembering lines by Clare, I'd sometimes rest
Contentful on the cushioned moss that grew
Between its roots. Finches, a flitting crew,
Chirped their concerns. Wiltshire, from east to west
Contained my tree. And Edmund never guessed
How he was there with me till dusk and dew.

Thus, fancy-free from ownership and claim,
The mind can make its legends live and sing
And grow to be the genius of some place.
And thus, where sylvan shadows held a name,
The thought of Poetry will dwell, and bring
To summer's idyll an unheeded grace.

Siegfried Sassoon

Bog oak

A carter's trophy
split for rafters,
a cobwebbed, black,
long-seasoned rib

under the first thatch.
I might tarry
with the moustached
dead, the creel-fillers,

or eavesdrop on
their hopeless wisdom
as a blow-down of smoke
struggles over the half-door

and mizzling rain
blurs the far end
of the cart track.
The softening ruts

lead back to no
'oak groves', no
cutters of mistletoe
in the green clearings.

Perhaps I just make out
Edmund Spenser,
dreaming sunlight,
encroached upon by

geniuses who creep
'out of every corner
of the woodes and glennes'
towards watercress and carrion.

Seamus Heaney

'The bushy leafy oak tree'

The bushy leafy oak tree
is highest in the wood,
the forking shoots of hazel
hide sweet hazel-nuts.

The alder is my darling,
all thornless in the gap,
some milk of human kindness
coursing in its sap.

The blackthorn is a jaggy creel
stippled with dark sloes;
green watercress in thatch on wells
where the drinking blackbird goes.

Sweetest of the leafy stalks,
the vetches strew the pathway;
the oyster-grass is my delight,
and the wild strawberry.

Low-set clumps of apple trees
drum down fruit when shaken;
scarlet berries clot like blood
on mountain rowan.

Briars curl in sideways,
arch a stickle back,
draw blood and curl up innocent
to sneak the next attack.

The yew tree in each churchyard
wraps night in its dark hood.
Ivy is a shadowy
genius of the wood.

Holly rears its windbreak,
a door in winter's face;
life-blood on a spear-shaft
darkens the grain of ash.

Birch tree, smooth and blessed,
delicious to the breeze,
high twigs plait and crown it
the queen of trees.

The aspen pales
and whispers, hesitates:
a thousand frightened scuts
race in its leaves.

But what disturbs me most
in the leafy wood
is the to and fro and to and fro
of an oak rod.

                    trans. *Seamus Heaney*
                    from Sweeney Astray

Cardiff Elms

Until this summer
through the open roof of the car
their lace was light as rain
against the burning sun.
On a rose-coloured road
they laid their inks,
knew exactly, in the seed,
where in the sky they would reach
precise parameters.

Traffic-jammed under a square
of perfect blue I thirst
for their lake's fingering
shadow, trunk by trunk arching
a cloister between the parks
and pillars of a civic architecture,
older and taller than all of it.

Heat is a salt encrustation.
Walls square up to the sky
without the company of leaves
or the town life of birds.
At the roadside this enormous
firewood, elmwood, the start
of some terrible undoing.

Gillian Clarke

The Cedar

Look from the high window with the eye of wonder
When the sun soars over and the moon dips under.

Look when the sun is coming and the moon is going
On the aspiring creature, on the cedar growing.

Plant or world? are those lights and shadows
Branches, or great air-suspended meadows?

Boles and branches, haunted by the flitting linnet,
Or great hillsides rolling up to cliffs of granite?

Those doomed shapes, thick-clustered on the ledges,
Upright fruit, or dwellings thatched with sedges?

Fair through the eye of innocence returning,
This is a country hanging in the morning;

Scented alps, where nothing but the daylight changes,
Climbing to black walls of mountain ranges;

And under the black walls, under the sky-banners,
The dwellings of the blessed in the green savannahs.

Ruth Pitter

Ceremonies for Candlemasse Eve

Down with the Rosemary and Bayes,
    Down with the Mistleto;
In stead of Holly, now up-raise
    The greener Box (for show.)

The Holly hitherto did sway;
    Let Box now domineere;
Untill the dancing Easter-day,
    Or Easters Eve appeare.

Then youthfull Box which now hath grace,
    Your houses to renew;
Grown old, surrender must his place,
    Unto the crisped Yew.

When Yew is out, then Birch comes in,
    And many Flowers beside;
Both of a fresh, and fragrant kinne
    To honour Whitsontide.

Green Rushes then, and sweetest Bents,
    With cooler Oken boughs;
Come in for comely ornaments,
    To re-adorn the house.
Thus times do shift; each thing his turne do's hold;
New things succeed, as former things grow old.

                   Robert Herrick

The Chalk-Pit

'Is this the road that climbs above and bends
Round what was once a chalk-pit: now it is
By accident an amphitheatre.
Some ash trees standing ankle-deep in brier
And bramble act the parts, and neither speak
Nor stir.' 'But see: they have fallen, every one,
And brier and bramble have grown over them.'
'That is the place. As usual no one is here.
Hardly can I imagine the drop of the axe,
And the smack that is like an echo, sounding here.'
'I do not understand.' 'Why, what I mean is
That I have seen the place two or three times
At most, and that its emptiness and silence
And stillness haunt me, as if just before
It was not empty, silent, still, but full
Of life of some kind, perhaps tragical.
Has anything unusual happened here?'

'Not that I know of. It is called the Dell.
They have not dug chalk here for a century.
That was the ash trees' age. But I will ask.'
'No. Do not. I prefer to make a tale,
Or better leave it like the end of a play,
Actors and audience and lights all gone;
For so it looks now. In my memory

Again and again I see it, strangely dark,
And vacant of a life but just withdrawn.
We have not seen the woodman with the axe.
Some ghost has left it now as we two came.'

'And yet you doubted if this were the road?'
'Well, sometimes I have thought of it and failed
To place it. No. And I am not quite sure,
Even now, this is it. For another place,
Real or painted, may have combined with it.
Or I myself a long way back in time. . .'
'Why, as to that, I used to meet a man—
I had forgotten,—searching for birds' nests
Along the road and in the chalk-pit too.
The wren's hole was an eye that looked at him
For recognition. Every nest he knew.
He got a stiff neck, by looking this side or that,
Spring after spring, he told me, with his laugh,—
A sort of laugh. He was a visitor,
A man of forty,—smoked and strolled about.
At orts and crosses Pleasure and Pain had played
On his brown features;—I think both had lost;—
Mild and yet wild too. You may know the kind.
And once or twice a woman shared his walks,
A girl of twenty with a brown boy's face,
And hair brown as a thrush or as a nut,
Thick eyebrows, glinting eyes—' 'You have said enough.
A pair,—free thought, free love,—I know the breed:
I shall not mix my fancies up with them.'

'You please yourself. I should prefer the truth
Or nothing. Here, in fact, is nothing at all
Except a silent place that once rang loud,
And trees and us—imperfect friends, we men
And trees since time began; and nevertheless
Between us still we breed a mystery.'

Edward Thomas

The Cherry Tree

In her gnarled sleep it
begins
      though she seems
as unmoving as the statue
of a running man: her
branches caught in a
writhing, her trunk
leaning as if in mid-fall.
When the wind moves
against her grave body
only the youngest twigs
scutter amongst themselves.

But there's something going on
in those twisted brown limbs,
it starts as a need
and it takes over, a need
to push
      push outward
from the center, to
bring what is not
from what is, pushing
till at the tips of the push
something comes about
             and then
pulling it from outside
until yes she has them started
tiny bumps
appear at the ends of twigs.

Then at once they're all here,
she wears them like a coat
a coat of babies,
I almost think that she
preens herself, jubilant at
the thick dazzle of bloom,

that the caught writhing has become
a sinuous wriggle of joy
beneath her fleece.
But she is working still
to feed her children,
there's a lot more yet,
bringing up all she can
a lot of goodness from roots

while the petals drop.
The fleece is gone
as suddenly as it came
and hundreds of babies are left
almost too small to be seen
but they fatten, fatten, get pink
and shine among her leaves.

Now she can repose a bit
they are so fat.
                    She cares less
birds get them, men
pick them, human children wear them
in pairs over their ears
she loses them all.
That's why she made them,
to lose them into the world, she
returns to herself,
she rests, she doesn't care.

She leans into the wind
her trunk shines black
with rain, she sleeps
as black and hard as lava.
She knows nothing about babies.

Thom Gunn

The Cherry Trees

The cherry trees bend over and are shedding,
On the old road where all that passed are dead,
Their petals, strewing the grass as for a wedding
This early May morn when there is none to wed.

Edward Thomas

The Christmas Tree

Put out the lights now!
Look at the Tree, the rough tree dazzled
In oriole plumes of flame,
Tinselled with twinkling frost fire, tasselled
With stars and moons—the same
That yesterday hid in the spinney and had no fame
Till we put out the lights now.

Hard are the nights now:
The fields at moonrise turn to agate,
Shadows are cold as jet;
In dyke and furrow, in copse and faggot
The frost's tooth is set;
And stars are the sparks whirled out by the north wind's fret
On the flinty nights now.

So feast your eyes now
On mimic star and moon-cold bauble:
Worlds may wither unseen,
But the Christmas Tree is a tree of fable,
A phoenix in evergreen,
And the world cannot change or chill what its mysteries
    mean
To your hearts and eyes now.

The vision dies now
Candle by candle: the tree that embraced it
Returns to its own kind,
To be earthed again and weather as best it
May the frost and the wind.
Children, it too had its hour—you will not mind
If it lives or dies now.

C. Day Lewis

The Combe

The Combe was ever dark, ancient and dark.
Its mouth is stopped with bramble, thorn, and briar;
And no one scrambles over the sliding chalk
By beech and yew and perishing juniper
Down the half precipices of its sides, with roots
And rabbit holes for steps. The sun of Winter,
And moon of Summer, and all the singing birds
Except the missel-thrush that loves juniper,
Are quite shut out. But far more ancient and dark
The Combe looks since they killed the badger there,
Dug him out and gave him to the hounds,
That most ancient Briton of English beasts.

Edward Thomas

'Come, farmers, then, and learn the form of tendance'

. . .Come, farmers, then, and learn the form of tendance
Each kind of tree requires; domesticate
The wild by culture. Do not let your land

Lie idle. O what joy to plant with vines
All Ismarus and clothe the great Taburnus
With olives! . . .
                            . . . The moral is
That every tree needs labour, all must be
Forced into furrows, tamed at any cost.
But olives favour truncheons, vines come best
From layers, myrtles best from solid stems,
From suckers hardy hazels, and from seed
The mighty ash, the shady tree whose leaves
Hercules plucked to crown him, and the acorns
Of the Chaonian Father. Likewise spring
From seed the lofty palm tree and the fir
Destined to see the hazards of the deep.
Grafting it is that makes the rugged arbute
Bear walnuts, barren planes rear healthy apples
And chestnuts foster beeches; thanks to this
The manna-ash can blanch with pear-blossom
And pigs munch acorns at the elm tree foot.
    The arts of budding and of grafting differ.
In the former, where the buds push out of the bark
And burst their delicate sheaths, just in the knot,
A narrow slit is made. In this an eye
From an alien tree is set and taught to merge
Into the sappy rind.
In the latter, knotless trunks are trimmed, and there
Wedges are driven deep into the wood,
Then fertile slips inserted. Presently
Up shoots a lofty tree with flourishing boughs,
Marvelling at its unfamiliar leaves
And fruits unlike its own. . . .

Virgil
from The Georgics Book II

The Crab Tree

Here is the crab tree,
Firm and erect,
In spite of the thin soil,
In spite of neglect.
The twisted root grapples
For sap with the rock,
And draws the hard juice
To the succulent top:
Here are wild apples,
Here's a tart crop!

No outlandish grafting
That ever grew soft
In a sweet air of Persia,
Or safe Roman croft;
Unsheltered by steading,
Rock-rooted and grown,
A great tree of Erin,
It stands up alone,
A forest tree spreading
Where forests are gone.

Of all who pass by it
How few in it see
A westering remnant
Of days when Lough Neagh
Flowed up the long dingles
Its blossom had lit,
Old days of glory
Time cannot repeat;
And therefore it mingles
The bitter and sweet.

It takes from the West Wind
The thrust of the main;
It makes from the tension

Of sky and of plain,
Of what clay enacted,
Of living alarm,
A vitalised symbol
Of earth and of storm,
Of Chaos contracted
To intricate form.

Unbreakable wrestler!
What sapling or herb
Has core of such sweetness
And fruit so acerb?
So grim a transmitter
Of life through mishap,
That one wonders whether
If that in the sap,
Is sweet or is bitter
Which makes it stand up.

Oliver St. John Gogarty

Cypress & Cedar

A smell comes off my pencil as I write
in the margins of a sacred Sanskrit text.
By just sufficient candlelight I skim
these scriptures sceptically from hymn to hymn.
The bits I read aloud to you I've Xed
for the little clues they offer to life's light.

I sit in mine, and you sit in your chair.
A sweetness hangs round yours; a foul smell mine.
Though the house still has no windows and no doors
and the tin roof's roughly propped with 4 x 4s
that any gale could jolt, our chairs are fine
and both scents battle for the same night air.

Near Chiefland just off US 129,
from the clapboard abattoir about a mile,
the local sawyer Bob displays his wares:
porch swings, picnic tables, lounging chairs,
rough sawn and nailed together 'cracker' style.
The hand I shake leaves powerful smells on mine.

Beside two piles of shavings, white and red,
one fragrant as a perfume, and one rank
and malodorous from its swampland ooze,
Bob displayed that week's work's chairs for me to choose.
I chose one that was sweet, and one that stank,
and thought about the sweet wood for a bed.

To quote the carpenter he 'stinks o' shite'
and his wife won't sleep with him on cypress days,
but after a day of cedar, so he said,
she comes back eagerly into his bed,
and, as long as he works cedar, there she stays.
Sometimes he scorns the red wood and works white!

Today I've laboured with my hands for hours
sawing fenceposts up for winter; one tough knot
jolted the chainsaw at my face and sprayed
a beetroot cedar dust off the bucked blade,
along with damp earth with its smell of rot,
hurtling beetles, termites in shocked showers.

To get one gatepost free I had to tug
for half an hour, but dragged up from its hole
it smelled, down even to the last four feet
rammed in the ground, still beautifully sweet
as if the grave had given life parole
and left the sour earth perfumed where I'd dug.

Bob gave me a cedar buckle for my belt,
and after the whole day cutting, stacking wood,
damp denim, genitals, 'genuine hide leather'

all these fragrances were bound together
by cedar, and together they smelled good.
It was wonderful the way my trousers smelled.

I can't help but suppose flesh-famished Phèdre
would have swept this prissy, epicene,
big-game hunting stepson Hippolyte,
led by his nose to cedar, off his feet,
and left no play at all for poor Racine,
if she'd soaped her breasts with *Bois de Cèdre*,

If in doubt ask Bob the sawyer's wife!
Pet lovers who can't stand the stink of cat
buy sacks of litter that's been 'cedarized'
and from ancient times the odour's been much prized.
Though not a Pharaoh I too favour that
for freighting my rank remains out of this life.

Why not two cedar chairs? Why go and buy
a reeking cypress chair as a reminder,
as if one's needed, of primeval ooze,
like swamps near Suwannee backroads, or bayous,
stagnation Mother Nature left behind her
hauling Mankind up from mononuclei?

Cypress still has roots in that old stew
paddling its origins in protozoa,
the stew where consciousness that writes and reads
grew its first squat tail from slimy seeds.
I'd've used it for the Ark if I'd been Noah,
though cedar, I know you'll say, would also do.

This place not in the *Blue Guide* or in *Fodor*
between the Suwannee River and the Styx
named by some homesick English classicist
who loved such puns, loathed swamps, and, lonely, pissed
his livelihood away with redneck hicks
and never once enjoyed the cedar's odour,

55

or put its smoke to snake-deterrent use
prescribed by Virgil in his *Georgics* III
with *chelydrus* here in the US south
construed as the diamondback or cottonmouth
which freed him, some said, from his misery.
Others said liquor, and others still a noose.

And, evenings, he, who'd been an avid reader
of the *Odyssey* and the *Iliad* in Greek,
became an even avider verandah drinker
believing sourmash made a Stoic thinker
though stuck with no paddle up Phlegethon's creek,
and had no wife with clothes chest of sweet cedar.

But you bought one at Bob's place and you keep
your cotton frocks in it, your underwear,
and such a fragrance comes from your doffed bras
as come from uncorked phials in hot bazaars,
and when you take your clothes off and lie bare
your body breathes out cedar while you sleep.

That lonely English exile named the river,
though it could have been someone like me, for whom,
though most evenings on the porch I read and write,
there's often such uneasiness in night
it creates despair in me, or drinker's gloom
that could send later twinges through the liver.

Tonight so far's been peaceful with no lightning.
The pecan trees and hophornbeams are still.
The storm's held off, the candleflame's quite straight,
the fire and wick united in one fate.
Though this quietness that can, one moment, fill
the heart with peace, can, the next, be frightening—

A hog gets gelded with a gruesome squeal
that skids across the quietness of night
to where we're sitting on our dodgy porch.

I reach for Seth Tooke's shotgun and the torch
then realize its 'farmwork' so alright
but my flesh also flinches from the steel.

Peace like a lily pad on swamps of pain—
floating's its only way of being linked.
This consciousness of ours that reads and writes
drifts on a darkness deeper than the night's.
Above that blackness, buoyed on the extinct,
peace, pure-white, floats flowering in the brain,

and fades, as finally the nenuphar
we found on a pewter swamp where two roads ended
was also bound to fade. The head and heart
are neither of them too much good apart
and peace comes in the moments that they're blended
as cypress and cedar at this moment are.

My love, as prone as I am to despair,
I think the world of night's best born in pairs,
one half we'll call the female, one the male,
though neither essence need, in love, prevail.
We sit here in distinctly scented chairs
you, love, in the cedar, me the cypress chair.

Though tomorrow night I might well sit in yours
and you in mine, the blended scent's the same
since I pushed my chair close to your chair
and we read by the one calm candle that we share
in this wilderness that might take years to tame,
this house still with no windows and no doors.

Let the candle cliché come out of the chill—
'the flickering candle on a vast dark plain'
of one lone voice against the state machine,
or Mimi's on cold stairs aren't what I mean
but moments like this now when heart and brain
seem one sole flame that's bright and straight and still.

If it's in Levy County that I die
(though fearing I'd feel homesick as I died
I'd sooner croak in Yorkshire if I could)
I'll have my coffin made of cedar wood
to balance the smell like cypress from inside
and hope the smoke of both blends in the sky,

as both scents from our porch chairs do tonight.
'Tvashti', says this Indian Rig Veda,
'hewed the world out of one tree,' but doesn't tell,
since for durability both do as well,
if the world he made was cypress wood; or cedar
the smell coming off my pencil as I write.

Tony Harrison

Dead Wood

Worn down to stumps, shredded by the wind,
Crushed underfoot in brittle slaty husks,
The forest turned from wood to stone to dust.

The rind of bark peeled off in slivers, shed
Dry spores, mineral resins, scales of scrim,
Scattering huge-leaved branches under the sun.

These giants shrank to pygmies in the glare.
Basilisks flashed their petrifying eyes.
The whole plateau rattled with bones of trees.

Now oil-men bring the few gnarled timbers back
As souvenirs. A lopped stone branch lies there
To hold up books, or prop open a door.

Anthony Thwaite

Delight of Being Alone

I know no greater delight than the sheer delight of being alone
It makes me realise the delicious pleasure of the moon
that she has in travelling by herself: throughout time,
or the splendid growing of an ash-tree
alone, on a hill-side in the north, humming in the wind.

D. H. Lawrence

Dieback

Eyes register their natural frontiers
Over invisible marathons, snakes, grasses,
Retreating to familiarity,
Imagination, mind, my feet and shoes.
This is oceanic country and I want a horse
And to be lonely, lawless and nomadic.
Beneath the Australasian blue
On the Tablelands, the dry pasturage
Rises and falls on continental cadences.
A lifetime dreaming of summers in Scotland
Brings me a big bag of blue childhood
But this is more of sky, an up-above
Illusory with yonder's blue beyond blue.
More birds enter my vocabulary
But I have no names by which to call them:
Eyes chronicle these things, all new to me,
Wordless in an optic archive.
I've seen the land and heard its native tongue,
But I'm its stranger, a pig-ignorant
Pedestrian, watching what he steps on.
Though I've been bumped into by a mad bat
With faulty radar, and bitten by a stoat
In Scotland, nature here is angrier
Than sanity can bear to contemplate.

I could do with grey-green gum-tree shade
And the perfumery of eucalypts,
But this is a landscape of dieback, trees
Whipped by bacterial artistry and flayed
Into nude postures, bark and leafage gone,
A famished gathering of naked Ys.
I can see five animals, including man
In a fast Japanese vehicle, spurting dust
With speed's up-tempo confidence.
Good State, what's stripped your forests bare,
What pastoral crime's been done to you
In this modernity, by carelessness
Or by sap-sipping, hungry beetles?
I haven't got the right, but I care.
Night falls here without sorrow. Truly, it falls
With howling innocence, cold and starry.
Under a slice of moon, the bald forests cry
Standing in their own coffins.

Douglas Dunn

Domus Caedet Arborem

Ever since the great planes were murdered at the end of the
    gardens
The city, to me, at night has the look of a Spirit brooding
    crime;
As if the dark houses watching the trees from dark windows
        Were simply biding their time.

Charlotte Mew

Elder

Feigns dead in winter, none lives better.
Chewed by cattle springs up stronger; an odd
Personal smell and unlovable skin;
Straight shoots like organ pipes in cigarette paper.
No nurseryman would sell you an
Elder—'not bush, not tree, not bad, not good'.
Judas was surely a fragile man
To hang himself from this—'God's stinking tree'.

In summer it juggles flower-plates in air,
Creamy as cumulus, and berries, each a weasel's eye
Of light. Pretends it's unburnable
(Who burns it sees the Devil), cringes, hides a soul
Of cream plates, purple fruits in a rattle
Of bones. A good example.

P. J. Kavanagh

The Elm

This is the place where Dorothea smiled.
I did not know the reason, nor did she.
But there she stood, and turned, and smiled at me:
A sudden glory had bewitched the child.
The corn at harvest, and a single tree.
This is the place where Dorothea smiled.

Hilaire Belloc

The Elm Beetle

So long I sat and conned
That naked bole
With the strange hieroglyphics scored
That those small priests,
The beetle-grubs, had bored,
Telling of gods and kings and beasts
And the long journey of the soul
Through magic-opened gates
To where the throned Osiris waits,
That when at last I woke
I stepped from an Egyptian tomb
To see the wood's sun-spotted gloom,
And rising cottage smoke
That leaned upon the wind and broke,
Roller-striped fields, and smooth cow-shadowed pond.

Andrew Young

The Elm Decline

The crags crash to the tarn; slow-
motion corrosion of scree.
From scooped corries,
bare as slag,
black sykes ooze
through quarries of broken boulders.
The sump of the tarn
slumps into its mosses—bog
asphodel, sundew, sedges—
a perpetual
sour October
yellowing the moor.

                                        Seven
thousand years ago
trees grew
high as this tarn. The pikes
were stacks and skerries
spiking the green,
the tidal surge
of oak, birch, elm,
ebbing to ochre
and the wrackwood of backend.

                                          Then
round the year Three
Thousand B.C.,
the proportion of elm pollen
preserved in peat
declined from twenty
per cent to four.

                              Stone axes,
chipped clean from the crag-face,
ripped the hide off the fells.
Spade and plough
scriated the bared flesh,
skewered down to the bone.
The rake flaked into fragments
and kettlehole tarns
were shovelled chock-full
of a rubble of rotting rocks.

                                   Today
electric landslips
crack the rock;
drills tunnel it;
valleys go under the tap.
Dynamited runnels
channel a poisoned rain,

and the fractured ledges
are scoured and emery'd
by wind-to-wind rubbings
of nuclear dust.

Soon
the pikes, the old
bottlestops of lava,
will stand scraped bare,
nothing but air round stone
and stone in air,
ground-down stumps
of a skeleton jaw—

Until
under the scree,
under the riddled rake,
beside the outflow of the reedless lake,
no human eye remains to see
a land-scape man
helped nature make.

Norman Nicholson

The Elms

Air darkens, air cools
And the first rain is heard in the great elms
A drop for each leaf, before it reaches the ground
I am still alive.

John Fuller

The Elm's Home

I

A dark sky blowing over
our backyard maples,
the air already cool,
Brockport begins its autumn.
My mower's drone and power
drift past the first leaves fallen
curled into red and yellow fists.
In a corner of lawn against
an old wire fence against the older woods,
a grove of mushrooms the kids
already hacked umbrellaless with golfclubs
rots into a mush of lumped columns,
pleats and fans.

These are the suburbs
where I loved that tree, our one elm.
Now, an inch under the loam,
its stump is a candle
of slow decay, lighting, above it,
thousands of perfect pearls
tiered like ant-eggs,
and these, by nature, growing so low
my mower's blades will never touch them.

II

My precious secrets come
to this, then? Yes.
Stay away from them,
you careless bastards.

But listen: sometimes,
at night, kneeling
within a dream within
the elm's oval shadow,

I can look down
into my leg-bones,
into my own marrow
clustered with eggs,

small and perfect pearl
mushrooms
living for all my life.
I can look up

into the elm and hear each leaf
whisper in my own breath, *welcome
home, this is your home,
welcome home.*

III

Sun, shine through me,
   for I have lost my body,
      my old elm gone home
   to its earthy city, O
sun, shine through me.

IV

Downward leader flash track
driving: 1,000 miles per second;
inconceivable return track:
87,000 miles per second.

But if we could stop it with our eyes:
its central core, hotter and brighter
than the surface of the sun,
only half-inch to an inch diameter;

its corona envelope, or glow discharge,
ten to twenty feet. Lightning:
our eyeballs' branched after-image. Lightning:
smell of ozone in the air,

pure stroke and electric numen.

V

Last night, heat
lightning branching
the blue-black sky,
alone on our back lawn,
when I closed my eyes for the right time,
when I knelt within the nimbus
where the elm I loved
lived for a hundred years,

when I touched the loam fill over the elm's stump,
its clusters of tiny noctilucent mushrooms,
I saw through them
into the ground, into the elm's dead
luminous roots, the branches of heaven
under the earth, this island home,
my lightning lord,
my home.

William Heyen

Elms under Cloud

Elms, old men with thinned-out hair,
And mouths down-turned, express
The oldness of the English scene:

And up the hill a pale road reaches
To a huge paleness browned with scattered,
Irritated cloud.

The spirit takes the chalky road, and says,
When will the clouds, like curves of love
Above the scene, again be smoothly rolled?

Geoffrey Grigson

Ending up in Kent

I'm leaning out the cottage window, latch
unfastened, trying to see for miles, further.
Postcard-picture me in a country of thatch,
twisted lanes, daub and wattle. I entertain
with coal-fires and gas cylinders.
For all through the year it rains, I freeze.
The neighboring oasts are like spindles,
fat with the wound-up thread of absent summer.
I walk detergent streams, in search of trees.

Someone's put me in a story-book, but kills
every tree before my entrance.
I follow an ordnance map and find
frightening rows of straight and vacant pines.
The earth as barren as the rugs
people in my nearby town put down. Medicine
sting of pine. Listen there, hear nothing. No bird sings.
I'm told that insects are the only living things
in that Forestry Commission flat. And slugs.

Gala-day on the Tonbridge-Hastings line
and my landlord's chopping down his chestnut trees.
Two train stops and you're at a famous Waters place
where they renovate shops into postcard prints.

Inside are offices, outside a show of wealth. In me,
when I walk that scenic, cobbled walk, a tall tree
grows crooked, like a money-graph
zigzagging into civic failure. In warm weather
they sell sulphur from the Wells for your pleasure.
Good Health! November and the Guy will burn.
What leaves are left on what trees are left will turn.

Eva Salzman

An English Wood

This valley wood is pledged
To the set shape of things,
And reasonably hedged:
Here are no harpies fledged,
No rocs may clap their wings,
Nor gryphons wave their stings.
Here, poised in quietude,
Calm elementals brood
On the set shape of things:
They fend away alarms
From this green wood.
Here nothing is that harms—
No bulls with lungs of brass,
No toothed or spiny grass,
No tree whose clutching arms
Drink blood when travellers pass,
No mount of glass;
No bardic tongues unfold
Satires or charms.
Only, the lawns are soft,
The tree-stems, grave and old;
Slow branches sway aloft,
The evening air comes cold,

The sunset scatters gold.
Small grasses toss and bend,
Small pathways idly tend
Towards no fearful end.

Robert Graves

'Enter these enchanted woods'

I

Enter these enchanted woods,
        You who dare.
Nothing harms beneath the leaves
More than waves a swimmer cleaves.
Toss your heart up with the lark,
Foot at peace with mouse and worm,
        Fair you fare.
Only at a dread of dark
Quaver, and they quit their form:
Thousand eyeballs under hoods
        Have you by the hair.
Enter these enchanted woods,
        You who dare.

II

Here the snake across your path
Stretches in his golden bath:
Mossy-footed squirrels leap
Soft as winnowing plumes of Sleep:
Yaffles on a chuckle skim
Low to laugh from branches dim:
Up the pine, where sits the star,
Rattles deep the moth-winged jar.

Each has business of his own;
But should you distrust a tone,
　　　Then beware.
Shudder all the haunted roods,
All the eyeballs under hoods
　　　Shroud you in their glare.
Enter these enchanted woods,
　　　You who dare.

George Meredith
from The Woods of Westermain

The Fallen Elm

Old elm, that murmured in our chimney top
The sweetest anthem autumn ever made
And into mellow whispering calms would drop
When showers fell on thy many coloured shade
And when dark tempests mimic thunder made—
While darkness came as it would strangle light
With the black tempest of a winter night
That rocked thee like a cradle in thy root—
How did I love to hear the winds upbraid
Thy strength without—while all within was mute.
It seasoned comfort to our hearts' desire,
We felt that kind protection like a friend
And edged our chairs up closer to the fire,
Enjoying comfort that was never penned.
Old favourite tree, thou'st seen time's changes lower,
Though change till now did never injure thee;
For time beheld thee as her sacred dower
And nature claimed thee her domestic tree.
Storms came and shook thee many a weary hour,
Yet stedfast to thy home thy roots have been;
Summers of thirst parched round thy homely bower
Till earth grew iron—still thy leaves were green.
The children sought thee in thy summer shade
And made their playhouse rings of stick and stone;

The mavis sang and felt himself alone
While in thy leaves his early nest was made,
And I did feel his happiness mine own,
Nought heeding that our friendship was betrayed,
Friend not inanimate—though stocks and stones
There are, and many formed of flesh and bones.
Thou owned a language by which hearts are stirred
Deeper than by a feeling clothed in word,
And speakest now what's known of every tongue,
Language of pity and the force of wrong.
What cant assumes, what hypocrites will dare,
Speaks home to truth and shows it what they are.
I see a picture which thy fate displays
And learn a lesson from thy destiny;
Self-interest saw thee stand in freedom's ways—
So thy old shadow must a tyrant be.
Thou'st heard the knave, abusing those in power,
Bawl freedom loud and then oppress the free;
Thou'st sheltered hypocrites in many a shower,
That when in power would never shelter thee.
Thou'st heard the knave supply his canting powers
With wrong's illusions when he wanted friends;
That bawled for shelter when he lived in showers
And when clouds vanished made thy shade amends—
With axe at root he felled thee to the ground
And barked of freedom—O I hate the sound
Time hears its visions speak,—and age sublime
Hath made thee a disciple unto time.
—It grows the cant term of enslaving tools
To wrong another by the name of right;
Thus came enclosure—ruin was its guide,
But freedom's cottage soon was thrust aside
And workhouse prisons raised upon the site.
Een nature's dwellings far away from men,
The common heath, became the spoiler's prey;
The rabbit had not where to make his den

And labour's only cow was drove away.
No matter—wrong was right and right was wrong,
And freedom's bawl was sanction to the song.
—Such was thy ruin, music-making elm;
The right of freedom was to injure thine:
As thou wert served, so would they overwhelm
In freedom's name the little that is mine.
And there are knaves that brawl for better laws
And cant of tyranny in stronger power
Who glut their vile unsatiated maws
And freedom's birthright from the weak devour.

John Clare

Felling a Tree

The surge of spirit that goes with using an axe,
The first heat—and calming down till the stiff back's
Unease passed, and the hot moisture came on body.
There under banks of Dane and Roman with the golden
Imperial coloured flower, whose name is lost to me—
Hewing the trunk desperately with upward strokes;
Seeing the chips fly—(it was at shoulder height, the trunk)
The green go, and the white appear—
Who should have been making music, but this had to be done
To earn a cottage shelter, and milk, and a little bread:
To right a body, beautiful as water and honour could make one—
And like the soldier lithe of body in the foremost rank
I stood there, muscle stiff, free of arm, working out fear.
Glad it was the ash tree's hardness not of the oaks', of the iron
     oak.
Sweat dripped from me—but there was no stay and the echoing
     bank
Sent back sharp sounds of hacking and of true straight woodcraft.
Some Roman from the pinewood caught memory and laughed.

73

Hit, crack and false aim, echoed from the amphitheatre
Of what was Rome before Romulus drew shoulder of Remus
Nearer his own—or Fabius won his salvation of victories.
In resting I thought of the hidden farm and Rome's hidden mild
    yoke
Still on the Gloucester heart strong after love's fill of centuries,
For all the happy, or the quiet, Severn or Leadon streams.
Pondered on music's deep truth, poetry's form or metre,
Rested—and took a thought and struck onward again,
Who had frozen by Chaulnes out of all caring of pain—
Learnt Roman fortitude at Laventie or Ypres,
Saw bright edge bury dull in the beautiful wood,
Touched splinters so wonderful—half through and soon to come
    down
From that ledge of rock under harebell, the yellow flower—the
    pinewood's crown.
Four inches more—and I should hear the crash and great thunder
Of an ash Crickley had loved for a century, and kept her own.
Thoughts of soldier and musician gathered to me
The desire of conquest ran in my blood, went through me—
There was a battle in my spirit and my blood shared it,
Maisemore—and Gloucester—bred me, and Cotswold reared it,
This great tree standing nobly in the July's day full light
Nearly to fall—my courage broke—and gathered—my breath
    feared it,
My heart—and again I struck, again the splinters and steel glinters
Dazzled my eyes—and the pain and the desperation and near
    victory
Carried me onwards—there were exultations and mockings sunward
Sheer courage, as of boat sailings in equinoctial unsafe squalls,
Stiffened my virtue, and the thing was done. No. Dropped my body,
The axe dropped—for a minute, taking breath, and gathering
    the greedy
Courage—looking for rest to the farm and grey loose-piled walls,
Rising like Troilus to the first word of 'Ready',
The last desperate onslaught—took the two inches of too steady
Trunk—on the rock edge it lurched, threatening my labouring life

(Nearly on me). Like Trafalgar's own sails imperiously moving to
   defeat
Across the wide sky unexpected glided and the high bank's pines
   and fell straight
Lower and lower till the crashing of the fellow trees made strife.
The thud of earth, and the full tree lying low in state,
With all its glory of life and sap quick in the veins. . .
Such beauty, for the farm fires and heat against chilly rains,
Golden glows in the kitchen from what a century made great. . .

The axe fell from my hand, and I was proud of my hand,
Crickley forgave, for her nobleness, the common fate of trees
As noble or more noble, the oak, the elm that is treacherous,
But dear for her cherishing to this beloved and this rocky land.
Over above all the world there, in a tired glory swerved there,
To a fall, the tree that for long had watched Wales glow strong,
Seen Severn, and farm, and Brecon, Black Mountains times
   without reckon.
And tomorrow would be fuel for the bright kitchen—for brown
   tea, against cold night.

                                                    Ivor Gurney

Fence Posts

   It might be that horses would be useful
   On a snowy morning to take the trail
   Down the ridge to visit Steve or Mike and
   Faster than going around the gravelled road by car.

   So the thought came to fence a part of the forest,
   Thin trees and clear the brush,
   Ron splits cedar rails and fenceposts
   On Black Sands Placer road where he gets
   These great old butt logs from the Camptonville sawmill

Why they can't use them I don't know—
They aren't all pecky.
He delivers, too, in a bread van
His grandfather drove in Seattle.

Sapwood posts are a little bit cheaper than heartwood.
I could have bought all heartwood from the start
But then I thought how it doesn't work
To always make a point of getting the best which is why
I sometimes pick out the worse and damaged looking fruit
And vegetables at the market because I know
I actually will enjoy them in any case but
Some people might take them as second choice
And feel sour about it all evening.

With sapwood fenceposts
You ought to soak to make sure they won't rot
In a fifty-five gallon drum with penta 10 to 1
Which is ten gallons of oil and a gallon of
Termite and fungus poison.
I use old crankcase oil to dilute
And that's a good thing to do with it but,
There's not really enough old crank to go around.
The posts should be two feet in the ground.

So, soaking six posts a week at a time
The soaked pile getting bigger week by week,
But the oil only comes up one and a half feet.
I could add kerosene in
At seventy cents a gallon
Which is what it costs when you buy it by the drum
And that's $3.50 to raise the soaking level up
Plus a half a can of penta more, six dollars,
For a hundred and twenty fence posts
On which I saved thirty dollars by getting the sapwood,
But still you have to count your time,

A well-done fence is beautiful.
And horses, too.
Penny wise pound foolish either way.

Gary Snyder

Fifty Faggots

There they stand, on their ends, the fifty faggots
That once were underwood of hazel and ash
In Jenny Pinks's Copse. Now, by the hedge
Close packed, they make a thicket fancy alone
Can creep through with the mouse and wren. Next Spring
A blackbird or a robin will nest there,
Accustomed to them, thinking they will remain
Whatever is for ever to a bird:
This Spring it is too late; the swift has come.
'Twas a hot day for carrying them up:
Better they will never warm me, though they must
Light several Winters' fires. Before they are done
The war will have ended, many other things
Have ended, maybe, that I can no more
Foresee or more control than robin and wren.

Edward Thomas

'For over-al, wher that I myn eyen caste'

For over-al, wher that I myn eyen caste,
Were trees clad with leves that ay shal laste,
Eche in his kinde, of colour fresh and grene
As emeraude, that joye was to sene.

The bilder ook, and eek the hardy asshe;
The piler elm, the cofre unto careyne:
The boxtree piper; holm to whippes lasshe;
The sayling firr, the cipres, deth to pleyne;
The sheter ew, the asp for shaftes pleyne;
The olyve of pees, and eek the drunken vyne,
The victor palm, the laurer to devyne . . .

Geoffrey Chaucer
from The Parlement of Foules

'Give me a land of boughs in leaf'

Give me a land of boughs in leaf,
   A land of trees that stand;
Where trees are fallen, there is grief;
   I love no leafless land . . .

A. E. Housman

Glyn Cynon Wood

Aberdare, Llanwynno through,
all Merthyr to Llanfabon;
there was never a more disastrous thing
than the cutting of Glyn Cynon.

They cut down many a parlour pure
where youth and manhood meet;
in those days of the regular star
Glyn Cynon's woods were sweet.

If a man in sudden plight
took to flight from foe,
for guest-house to the nightingale
in Cynon Vale he'd go.

Many a birch-tree green of cloak
(I'd like to choke the Saxon!)
is now a flaming heap of fire
where iron-workers blacken.

For cutting the branch and bearing away
the wild birds' habitation
may misfortune quickly reach
Rowenna's treacherous children!

Rather should the English be
strung up beneath the seas,
keeping painful house in hell
than felling Cynon's trees.

Upon my oath, I've heard it said
that a herd of the red deer
for Mawddwy's deep dark woods has left,
bereft of its warmth here.

No more the badger's earth we'll sack
nor start a buck from the glade;
no more deer-stalking in my day,
now they've cut Glyn Cynon's shade.

If ever a stag got into a wood
with huntsmen a stride behind,
never again will he turn in his run
with Cynon Wood in mind.

If the flour-white girl once came
to walk along the brook,
Glyn Cynon's wood was always there
as a fair trysting nook.

If as in times gone by men plan
to span the mountain river;
though wood be found for house and church
Glyn Cynon's no provider.

I'd like to call on them a quest
of every honest bird,
where the owl, worthiest in the wood,
as hangman would be heard.

If there's a question who rehearsed
in verse this cruel tale,
it's one who many a tryst has kept
in the depth of Cynon Vale.

Anon

Green Man

Fleet in the forest,
leafshaken, wild in the wood,
flowers tousled in his hair,
garlanded with laurel and with ivy,
the Green Grotesque swoops out of stone and timber.
Locked in a church boss
his eyes start with alarm
at his enclosure. Brown priests agreed
to give his effigy a place.
That would bring the gaffers in,
the maids with May bandeaus,
the mothers full of fears and needing cures.
They could turn an eye
towards the old religion
while they received the new.
Christ nailed to a tree would keep their reverence
front facing; they could fringe
the altar of the new covenant with evergreen
with rosemary to sprig the nosegays left
under the wood-man's stare.

Needs are many and the winter cold,
best to placate all gods.
The Mediterranean Lord of Life
could promise them a warmer afterlife,
the Forest Sprite green leaves,
a yellow corn and a berried harvest.

Heather Harrison

Green Man in the Garden

Green man in the garden
  Staring from the tree,
Why do you look so long and hard
  Through the pane at me?

Your eyes are dark as holly,
  Of sycamore your horns,
Your bones are made of elder-branch,
  Your teeth are made of thorns.

Your hat is made of ivy-leaf,
  Of bark your dancing shoes,
And evergreen and green and green
  Your jacket and shirt and trews.

Leave your house and leave your land
  And throw away the key,
And never look behind, he creaked,
  And come and live with me.

I bolted up the window,
  I bolted up the door,
I drew the blind that I should find
  The green man never more.

But when I softly turned the stair
  As I went up to bed,
I saw the green man standing there.
  Sleep well, my friend, he said.

Charles Causley

'The groves are down'

The groves are down
           cut down
Groves of Ahab, of Cybele
Pine trees, knobbed twigs
    thick cone and seed
    Cybele's tree this, sacred in groves
Pine of Seami, cedar of Haida
Cut down by the prophets of Israel
    the fairies of Athens
    the thugs of Rome
          both ancient and modern;
Cut down to make room for the suburbs
Bulldozed by Luther and Weyerhaeuser
Crosscut and chainsaw
    squareheads and finns
    high-lead and cat-skidding
Trees down
Creeks choked, trout killed, roads.

Sawmill temples of Jehovah.
Squat black burners 100 feet high
Sending the smoke of our burnt
Live sap and leaf
To his eager nose.

Gary Snyder
from Logging

'The holly and the ivy'

The holly and the ivy,
When they are both full grown,
Of all the trees that are in the wood,
The holly bears the crown:

> *The rising of the sun*
> *And the running of the deer,*
> *The playing of the merry organ*
> *Sweet singing in the choir.*

The holly bears a blossom,
As white as the lily flower,
And Mary bore sweet Jesus Christ,
To be our sweet Saviour:

The holly bears a berry,
As red as any blood,
And Mary bore sweet Jesus Christ
To do poor sinners good:

The holly bears a prickle,
As sharp as any thorn,
And Mary bore sweet Jesus Christ
On Christmas day in the morn:

The holly bears a bark,
As bitter as any gall,
And Mary bore sweet Jesus Christ
For to redeem us all:

The holly and the ivy,
When they are both full grown,
Of all the trees that are in the wood,
The holly bears the crown:

Anon

Home-Thoughts, from Abroad

I
Oh, to be in England
Now that April's there,
And whoever wakes in England
Sees, some morning, unaware,
That the lowest boughs and the brushwood sheaf
Round the elm-tree bole are in tiny leaf,
While the chaffinch sings on the orchard bough
In England—now!

II
And after April, when May follows,
And the whitethroat builds, and all the swallows!
Hark, where my blossomed pear-tree in the hedge
Leans to the field and scatters on the clover
Blossoms and dewdrops—at the bent spray's edge—
That's the wise thrush; he sings each song twice over,
Lest you should think he never could recapture
The first fine careless rapture!

And though the fields look rough with hoary dew
All will be gay when noontide wakes anew
The buttercups, the little children's dower
—Far brighter than this gaudy melon-flower!

Robert Browning

'How long does it take to make the woods?'

How long does it take to make the woods?
As long as it takes to make the world.
The woods is present as the world is, the presence
of all its past, and of all its time to come.
It is always finished, it is always being made, the act
of its making forever greater than the act of its destruction.

It is a part of eternity, for its end and beginning
belong to the end and beginning of all things,
the beginning lost in the end, the end in the beginning.

What is the way to the woods, how do you go there?
By climbing up through the six days' field,
kept in all the body's years, the body's
sorrow, weariness, and joy. By passing through
the narrow gate on the far side of that field
where the pasture grass of the body's life gives way
to the high, original standing of the trees.
By coming into the shadow, the shadow
of the grace of the strait way's ending,
the shadow of the mercy of light.

Why must the gate be narrow?
Because you cannot pass beyond it burdened.
To come into the woods you must leave behind
the six days' world, all of it, all of its plans and hopes.
You must come without weapon or tool, alone,
expecting nothing, remembering nothing,
into the ease of sight, the brotherhood of eye and leaf.

Wendell Berry
from Sabbaths

'Hwaet! A dream came to me at deep midnight'

Hwaet!
A dream came to me
        at deep midnight
when humankind
        kept their beds
—the dream of dreams!
        I shall declare it.

It seemed I saw the Tree itself
borne on the air, light wound about it,
—a beam of brightest wood, a beacon clad
in overlapping gold, glancing gems
fair at its foot, and five stones
set in a crux flashed from the crosstree . . .

. . . Yet lying there a long while
I beheld, sorrowing, the Healer's Tree
till it seemed that I heard how it broke silence,
best of wood, and began to speak:

'Over that long remove my mind ranges
back to the holt where I was hewn down;
from my own stem I was struck away,
     dragged off by strong enemies,
wrought into a roadside scaffold.
     They made me a hoist for wrongdoers.

The soldiers on their shoulders bore me,
     until on a hill-top they set me up;
many enemies made me fast there.
     Then I saw, marching toward me,
mankind's brave King;
     He came to climb upon me.

I dared not break or bend aside
against God's will, though the ground itself
shook at my feet. Fast I stood,
who falling could have felled them all.

Almighty God ungirded Him,
     eager to mount the gallows,
unafraid in the sight of many:
     He would set free mankind.
I shook when His arms embraced me
     but I durst not bow to ground,
stoop to Earth's surface.
     Stand fast I must.

I was reared up, a rood.
        I raised the great King,
liege lord of the heavens,
        dared not lean from the true.
They drove me through with dark nails:
        on me are the deep wounds manifest,
wide-mouthed hate-dents.
                I durst not harm any of them.
How they mocked at us both!
        I was all moist with blood
sprung from the Man's side
        after He sent forth His soul.

Wry wierds a-many I underwent
up on that hill-top; saw the Lord of Hosts
stretched out stark. Darkness shrouded
the King's corse. Clouds wrapped
its clear shining. A shade went out
wan under cloud-pall. All creation wept,
keened the King's death. Christ was on the Cross . . .

Anon
from the Dream of the Rood

In a Wood

Pale beech and pine so blue,
        Set in one clay,
Bough to bough cannot you
        Live out your day?
When the rains skim and skip,
Why mar sweet comradeship,
Blighting with poison-drip
        Neighbourly spray?

Heart-halt and spirit-lame,
          City-opprest,
Unto this wood I came
          As to a nest;
Dreaming that sylvan peace
Offered the harrowed ease—
Nature a soft release
          From men's unrest.

But, having entered in,
          Great growths and small
Show them to men akin—
          Combatants all!
Sycamore shoulders oak,
Bines the slim sapling yoke,
Ivy-spun halters choke
          Elms stout and tall.

Touches from ash, O wych,
          Sting you like scorn!
You, too, brave hollies, twitch
          Sidelong from thorn.
Even the rank poplars bear
Lothly a rival's air,
Cankering in black despair
          If overborne.

Since, then, no grace I find
          Taught me of trees,
Turn I back to my kind,
          Worthy as these.
There at least smiles abound,
There discourse trills around,
There, now and then, are found
          Life-loyalties.

                    Thomas Hardy

'In midwinter a wood was'

In midwinter a wood was
where the sand-coloured deer ran
through quietness.
It was a marvellous thing
to see those deer running.

Softer than ashes
snow lay all winter where they ran,
and in the wood a holly tree was.
God, it was a marvellous thing
to see the deer running.

Between lime trunks grey or green
branch-headed stags went by
silently trotting.
A holly tree dark and crimson
sprouted at the wood's centre, thick and high
without a whisper, no other berry so fine.

Outside the wood was black midwinter,
over the downs that reared so solemn
wind rushed in gales, and strong here
wrapped around wood and holly fire
(where deer among the close limes ran)
with a storming circle of its thunder.
Under the trees it was a marvellous thing
to see the deer running.

Peter Levi

'In somer, when the shawes be sheyne'

In somer, when the shawes be sheyne
   And leves be large and long,
Hit is full mery in feyre foreste
   To here the foulys song;

To se the dere draw to the dale
   And leve the hilles hee,
And shadow hem in the leves grene
   Under the grene-wode tre . . .

Anon
from The Ballad of Robyn Hode
and the Munke

In the Woods

Always at this time there is the bankrupt plant:
autumn afflicts the failed machinery of ferns with rust.
The foliage is full of broken windows.
The birch trees shed their aluminium crust,

and the cedar drops its complicated cogs.
The roof of things has fallen in—
these paprika patches on the factory floor
are corrugated remnants of protective tin.

Oddments blacken strangely on a nearby fence:
rags, an old glove in a liquorice droop,
washleathers warp with dull black holly claws.
It is a sad, abandoned, oddly human group.

The glove is singular. You cannot try it on.
It is too small. Besides, it has no fingers.
It is more like something surgical—
the unpleasant shape of stumpy enigmas.

Below, a nylon sock curls up like a dead animal.
Through a hole in the toe, a glint of teeth.
Over there, the remains of a fire—
pigeon feathers in a narrow ashy wreath.

And everywhere egg-shells, egg-shells,
so light they stir with the gentlest breath—
a breakfast of papery skulls. The Omelette Man
has eaten here and manufactured death.

Craig Raine

In Westerham Woods

Two lovers here once carved their name,
A heart between them like a flame;
Now these two lovers' names depart
From either side a broken heart.

Andrew Young

'I saw in Louisiana a live-oak growing'

I saw in Louisiana a live-oak growing,
All alone stood it and the moss hung down from the
    branches,
Without any companion it grew there uttering joyous leaves
    of dark green,
And its look, rude, unbending, lusty, made me think of
    myself,
But I wonder'd how it could utter joyous leaves standing
    alone there without its friend near, for I knew I could not,
And I broke off a twig with a certain number of leaves upon
    it, and twined around it a little moss,

And brought it away, and I have placed it in sight in my
    room,
It is not needed to remind me as of my own dear friends,
(For I believe lately I think of little else than of them,)
Yet it remains to me a curious token, it makes me think of
    manly love;
For all that, and though the live-oak glistens there in
    Louisiana solitary in a wide flat space,
Uttering joyous leaves all its life without a friend a lover
    near,
I know very well I could not.

Walt Whitman

'I see the oak's bride in the oak's grasp'

I see the oak's bride in the oak's grasp.

Nuptials among prehistoric insects
The tremulous convulsion
The inching hydra strength
Among frilled lizards

Dropping twigs, and acorns, and leaves.
The oak is in bliss
Its roots
Lift arms that are a supplication
Crippled with stigmata
Like the sea-carved cliffs earth lifts
Loaded with dumb, uttering effigies
The oak seems to die and to be dead
In its love-act.

As I lie under it

In a brown leaf nostalgia

An acorn stupor.

Ted Hughes
from Gaudete

'I think that I shall never see'

I think that I shall never see
A poem as lovely as a tree,
Poems are made by fools like me
But only God can make a tree.

Alfred (Joyce) Kilmer

'It is not growing like a tree'

It is not growing like a tree
In bulk, doth make Man better be;
Or standing long an oak, three hundred year,

To fall a log at last, dry, bald, and sere:
A lily of a day
Is fairer far in May,
Although it fall and die that night;
It was the plant and flower of Light.
In small proportions we just beauties see;
And in short measures life may perfect be.

Ben Jonson

'The land of Y Llain was on the high marsh'

... The land of Y Llain was on the high marsh
on the border between Caron-is-Clawdd and Padarn Odwyn
slanting from Cae Top down to Y Waun,
and beyond Cae Top was a glade of dark trees—
pines and tall larches—to break the cold wind,
the wind from the north.
And there were the small four-sided fields
like checkerboard, or a patchwork quilt,
and around each of the fields, a hedge.

My father planted the hedges farthest from the house, —
the hedges of Cae Top and Cae Brwyn, —
myself a youngster at his heels
putting the plants in his hand:
three hawthorns and a beech-tree,
three hawthorns and a beech-tree in turn;
his feet measuring the distance between them along the top of the
    ditch,
squeezing them solidly into the loose earth-and-chalk.
Then the patterned wiring outside them—
the square posts of peeled oak-wood
sunk deep in the living earth—
and I getting to turn the wiring-engine on the post
while he did the stapling,
the hammer ringing in my ears with the pounding.
And I daring on the sly
to send a telegram back over the taut wires
to the other children at the far end of the ditch,
the note of music raising its pitch
with each turn I gave the old wiring-engine's handle.
My grandfather, said my father, had planted the Middle Fields
    —Cae Cwteri, Cae Polion, Cae Troi—
but generations we knew nothing at all about,
except for the mark of their handiwork on Cae Lloi and Cae Moch

had planted the tall strong stout-trunked trees round the house,
and set sweet-plums here and there in the hedges.
     And there we children would be
safe in a fold in the ditch under the hedges,
the dried leaves a coverlet to keep us warm
(like the babes in the story hidden with leaves by the birds).
The breeze that trickled through the trunks of the hedges
was not enough to ruffle the wren's and the robin's feathers:
but above the hedges and the trees, above the house,
aloft in the firmament, the wind was
tumbling the clouds, tickling them till their white laughter
was unruly hysteria like children on a kitchen floor,
till the excess of play turns suddenly strange
and the laughter's whiteness scowls, and darkens,
and the tears burst forth, and the clouds escape
in a race from the wind, from the tickling and the tumbling,
escaping headlong from the wind's provocation—
the pursuing wind outside me,
and I fast in the fold in the ditch beneath the leaves
listening to its sound, outside,
with nothing at all occuring within what I am
because of the care and craft of generations of my fathers
planting their hedges prudently to shelter me in my day,—
nothing—despite my wishing and wishing . . .

J. Kitchener Davies
from The Sound of the Wind that is Blowing

The Leaf

'How beautifully it falls,' you said,
As a leaf turned and twirled
On invisible wind upheld,
How airily to ground
Prolongs its flight.

You for a leaf-fall forgot
Old age, loneliness,
Body's weary frame,
Crippled hands, failing sense,
Unkind world and its pain.

What did that small leaf sign
To you, troth its gold
Plight 'twixt you and what unseen
Messenger to the heart
From a fair, simple land?

Kathleen Raine

'Living a good way up a mountain'

. . . Living a good way up a mountain
Above the natural line of trees,
We nurture saplings, ache for torn
Or wounded cedar, oak or thorn
And mourn fatalities.

Trees are annual calendars
And their expressive flags have taught us
To greet the spring. They're twiggy babels
For many birds; pencils and tables
To please our daughters' daughters.

The lifetime that they take to grow
Is rarely ours. We feel a bond
Like that with age: memorabilia
To be respected, grave, familiar,
A little feared or fond.

We note the fruiting of the rowan,
If it's the year for bullace or
For sloe, or how much higher stand
The valiant Blackheath walnut and
The Oxford sycamore.

But most regret in this last winter
The passing of an ancient ash
Which air, that changed location at
Unlikely speed, disturbed and flat-
tened with an unheard crash.

But now, although it leans upon
One hinge of bark, new leafage shoots
From stumps the guilty wind has healed.
It dipped its elbows in the field
And there established roots.

If only our unrooted lives
When felled could simply change direction
And all our tall assumptions both
Be trimmed and find amazing growth,
A perfect resurrection!

The tree has found a way of walking
Not as our childhood stories told us
Through sudden supernatural strength
But through first tumbling its full length
Then growing from its shoulders. . . .

John Fuller
from The Grey and the Green

London Trees

Out of the roads of London springs the forest,
Over and underworld, the veritable Eden
Here we have planted for our solitude,
Those planes, where thoughts unblamed among the leaves
    may run.

Sensing us, the trees tremble in their sleep,
The living leaves recoil before our fires.
Baring to us war-charred and broken branches,
And seeing theirs, we for our own destruction weep.

And women, sore at heart, trying to pray
Unravel the young buds with anxious fingers
Searching for God, who has gone far away,
Yet still at evening in the green world lingers.

Obedient still to Him, the toiling trees
Lift up their fountains, where still waters rise
Upwards into life, filled from the surrounding skies
To quench the sorrows thirsting in the world's eyes.

Kathleen Raine

The Long-Tailed Tits

I stopped to hear it clear,
The sound of water tinkling near,
Although I knew no dowser could
Turn hazel-fork in that beech-wood.

Then on the high tree-tops
With rising runs and jerks and stops
Like water stones break into bits
Flowed the cascade of long-tailed tits.

Andrew Young

'Loveliest of trees, the cherry now'

Loveliest of trees, the cherry now
Is hung with bloom along the bough,
And stands about the woodland ride
Wearing white for Eastertide.

Now, of my threescore years and ten,
Twenty will not come again,
And take from seventy springs a score,
It only leaves me fifty more.

And since to look at things in bloom
Fifty springs are little room,
About the woodlands I will go
To see the cherry hung with snow.

> A.E Housman
> *from* A Shropshire Lad

The Magic Apple Tree

Sealed in rainlight one
November sleepwalking afternoon streets
I remembered Samuel Palmer's garden
Waterhouse in Shoreham, and at once
I knew: that the chill of wet
brown streets was no more literal
than the yellow he laid there against
his unnatural blue   because
together they worked upon me like
an icon   infantine

he called his vision / so it was
with the early makers of icons, who
worked humbly, choosing wood without resin.
They stilled their spirits before using the gold

99

and while the brightness held under the *kvass*
their colours too induced
the peculiar joy of abandoning restlessness

and now in streets where only white
mac or car metal catches the failing
light, if we sing of
the red and the blue and the texture of goat hair,
there is no deceit in our prophecy:
for even now our brackish waters can
be sweetened by a strange tree.

Elaine Feinstein

Maple and Starlings

Over my head, a maple fills with starlings
against the evening sky.
I won't move, I won't speak.
The maple will hold them as long as it does.

In a few seconds, the maple rising above me blossomed
with starlings. Darker than evening, darker than leaves,
they flew from nowhere to here for the first time.
I knew maple and starlings for the first time.

This evening, the maple above me turned to starlings.
A few moments, and everything was over, nothing
changed. The starlings flew from nowhere they remember.
The maple stands for nothing in the evening air.

How long had it been evening?
As long as starlings' shadows
were blowing through the maples.
As long as leaves were flying.

Over my head, a maple fills with evening,
releases flows of starlings,
or receives them,
wherever they came from, wherever they're going.

The maple growing into the evening above me fills
with starlings. For a few seconds, it's been as though
I've not been here to say *maple*, and *starlings*.
For a few seconds, the evening has darkened with starlings.

Someone has been dreaming: maple, starlings,
an evening second by second being its own darkness.
A maple rising in the dark air: Starlings
from nowhere to nowhere. A maple. Starlings.

William Heyen

Maple and Sumach

Maple and sumach down this autumn ride—
Look, in what scarlet character they speak!
For this their russet and rejoicing week
Trees spend a year of sunsets on their pride.
You leaves drenched with the lifeblood of the year—
What flamingo dawns have wavered from the east,
What eves have crimsoned to their toppling crest
To give the fame and transience that you wear!
Leaf-low he shall lie soon: but no such blaze
Briefly can cheer man's ashen, harsh decline;
His fall is short of pride, he bleeds within
And paler creeps to the dead end of his days.
O light's abandon and the fire-crest sky
Speak in me now for all who are to die!

C. Day Lewis

The May-Tree

As if when a man was striding on an errand
of adult importance requiring a brief-case
a scruffy child should slip her hand in his
and he be obliged to accept her and protect her,
like this, today, the may came in my mind:
the responsibility.
                    Though she's no child —
I've looked at her for eighteen years from the window
and she was already old when we came to this house.
Her hair straggles and one shoulder's
a little higher than the other,
result of the careless way she's been flail-cut.
She's fruitful—so-so. Fieldfares take their toll.
But she's had to be tough: she isn't beautiful.

She grows against the wire of the farmer's field,
a tree, definitely, having a naked
visible trunk unlike the opulent
Palmeresque bushes behind her in the pasture.
Now they, when they're in bloom, are radiant
they can cause temporary transmutations
even in computer-friendly minds.
But she even I, her nearest sister, hadn't much
thought about till one day when two men came by
and stopped the tractor with the flail, got down
and shook her about and looked her over,
Was it worthwhile to keep an aging haw?
and I found myself running and trying not to scream
trying to discover I who was always craven
authority to hold their wanton hands.

Who smiled reassurance. Just trimming.
They knew at once what was the matter,
had seen women taken in this way before.
Their smiles had more than a sprinkling of scorn.

You don't bring may blossom into the house!
Everyone's mother taught them that.
Don't be afraid, Mother, don't be afraid
if I bring it indoors inside my head
loving and learning the tree that is over-against me:
I'm so afraid they will cut the may-tree down.

We can't carry the world, heroic, cracking:
Atlas was a man's misguided myth.
But let's carry a clod each
link arms and lift up a spring language
bud and break out and bring in better times.

Kim Taplin

The Memorial Trees

Here in the public garden deep with shade
    The branches cluster, filtering the sun,
And as they sway, the gaining patterns fade
    Across the paths and steps, and from the gun

Set into concrete, pointing up, dull green,
    Where olive trees enclose it row on row.
Enlaced above the barrel like a screen
    Their leaves are grey and silver as they blow

As if intended to conceal its aim;
    But tags of metal gleam from every tree
Where bark encroaches on a soldier's name
    Dulled by the bitter moisture from the sea;

It wanders in the leaves and makes them stir.
    Dry leaves, and ancient on the victim's head
But hung with fruit, a pulse of what they were;
    Now they are turned to trees, the living dead,

Yielders before the wind, graspers for life,
    For ever rooted where they understood
The angel shrieking with the grafting knife
    When the bombardment splintered in the wood.

Then saplings, and the shovelfuls of earth
    And grieving fingers spreading tender roots
Again at others' hands. But this was birth,
    To plant their dying with life's attributes,

The anguish of the living here revealed;
    When every autumn of the monument
With each rich pressing of the fruit must yield
    A trickle bright as pain for nourishment.

Michael Vince

Never Tell

The saplings of the green-tipped birch
Draw my foot from bondage:
Let no boy know your secret!

Oak saplings in the grove
Draw my foot from its chain:
Tell no secret to a maid!

Anon

The New Tree

Planted a tree the afternoon before
what has become the first evening of autumn
(eucalyptus-spring in Australia),
wind dropped and clouds moved on, mid-August storms
seemingly gone. And now the moon, almost
at full, a thin-worn disk of beaten tawny
metal foil, or crumpled papery fallen
eucalyptus leaf, hovers above the hawthorn
and the bramble hedges, unkempt corner
of my northern garden, as I cross the lawn
to touch the newly planted tree, its short
rose-madder stems and glaucous foliage, once more,
and wonder if its roots can feel the draw
of the antipodes, the pull from that far shore;
confirm again that everything's in order,
and wish it well until tomorrow's dawn.

Ruth Fainlight

'No weekends for the gods now. Wars'

. . . No weekends for the gods now. Wars
flicker, earth licks its open sores,
fresh breakage, fresh promotions, chance
assassinations, no advance.
Only man thinning out his kind
sounds through the Sabbath noon, the blind
swipe of the pruner and his knife
busy about the tree of life . . .

Robert Lowell
from Waking Early Sunday Morning

No-man's Wood

Shall I have jealous thoughts to nurse,
When I behold a rich man's house?
Not though his windows, thick as stars,
    Number the days in every year;
I, with one window for each month,
    Am rich in four or five to spare.

But when I count his shrubberies,
His fountains there, and clumps of trees,
Over the palings of his park
    I leap with my primeval blood;
Down wild ravines to Ocean's rocks,
    Clean through the heart of No-man's Wood.

W. H. Davies

'Nor less attractive is the woodland scene'

Nor less attractive is the woodland scene,
Diversified with trees of ev'ry growth,
Alike, yet various. Here the gray smooth trunks
Of ash, or lime, or beech, distinctly shine,
Within the twilight of their distant shades;
There, lost behind a rising ground, the wood
Seems sunk and shorten'd to its topmost boughs.
No tree in all the grove but has its charms,
Though each its hue peculiar; paler some,
And of a wannish gray; the willow such
And poplar, that with silver lines his leaf,
And ash far-stretching his umbrageous arm;
Of deeper green the elm; and deeper still,
Lord of the woods, the long-surviving oak.
Some glossy-leav'd, and shining in the sun,
The maple, and the beech of oily nuts

Prolific, and the lime at dewy eve
Diffusing odours: not unnoted pass
The sycamore, capricious in attire,
Now green, now tawny, and, ere autumn yet
Have chang'd the woods, in scarlet honours bright.
O'er these, but far beyond (a spacious map
Of hill and valley interpos'd between),
The Ouse, dividing the well-water'd land,
Now glitters in the sun, and now retires,
As bashful, yet impatient to be seen.

William Cowper
from The Task

Not After Plutarch

'Comfort me with apples'

parallel lives of one mind in two climes
this is my present reality—
beginning with rivers running reflective water
with wind nearest comparison of spirit
and apple orchards of forgotten tribes
fruit trees grown gaunt and tall
the apples small tough-skinned as berries
rough but tendersweet to teeth
used to crack hazel nuts or the long-sheathed filbert

this from the equator is the far isle
of the blest the happiest immortal hyperboreans
now I am sure this haunting of apple-eating
and gathering long painted ladders baskets
and measures heaped up grass lumpy
with tumbled harvest is the childhood be-
ginning of the discovery of Avalon

where the sun sets and all those western clouds
and shadowy hills are stained with human dreams

forget the fright of Eden deep is the Vale
of Avalon with sleep and mellow apple fruitage

Mary Casey

'Now I am here, what thou wilt do with me'

. . . Now I am here, what thou wilt do with me
  None of my books will show:
I reade, and sigh, and wish I were a tree;
  For sure then I should grow
To fruit or shade: at least some bird would trust
Her household to me, and I should be just. . .

George Herbert
from The Temple (Affliction I)

'Now, my co-mates and brothers in exile'

Duke Senior: Now, my co-mates and brothers in exile,
Hath not old customs made this life more sweet
Than that of painted pomp? Are not these woods
More free from peril than the envious court!
Here feel we not the penalty of Adam,
The seasons' difference; as the icy fang
And churlish chiding of the winter's wind,
Which when it bites and blows upon my body,
Even till I shrink with cold, I smile and say
'This is no flattery; these are counsellors
That feelingly persuade me what I am'.

Sweet are the uses of adversity;
Which, like the toad, ugly and venomous,
Wears yet a precious jewel in his head;
And this our life, exempt from public haunt,
Finds tongues in trees, books in the running brooks,
Sermons in stones, and good in everything.
I would not change it.

William Shakespeare
from As You Like It

'O Rosalind! these trees shall be my books'

Orlando: O Rosalind! these trees shall be my books,
And in their barks my thoughts I'll character,
That every eye which in this forest looks
Shall see thy virtue witness'd everywhere.
Run, run, Orlando; carve on every tree,
The fair, the chaste, and unexpressive she.

William Shakespeare
from As You Like It

Oak

Slow in growth, late in putting out leaves,
And the full leaves dark, austere,
Neither the flower nor the fruit sweet
Save to the harsh jay's tongue, squirrel's and boar's,
Oak has an earthward urge, each bough dithers,
Now rising, now jerked aside, twisted back,
Only the bulk of the lower trunk keeps
A straight course, only the massed foliage together
Rounds a shape out of knots and zigzags.

But when other trees, even the late-leaved ash,
Slow-growing walnut, wide-branching beech and linden
Sway in a summer wind, poplar and willow bend,
Oak alone looks compact, in a stillness hides
Black stumps of limbs that blight or blast bared;
And for death reserves its more durable substance.

On wide floorboards four centuries old,
Sloping, yet scarcely worn, I can walk
And in words not oaken, those of my time, diminished,
Mark them that never were a monument
But plain utility, and mark the diminution,
Loss of that patient tree, loss of the skills
That matched the patience, shaping hard wood
To outlast the worker and outlast the user;
How by oak beams, worm-eaten,
This cottage stands, when brick and plaster have crumbled,
In casements of oak the leaded panes rest
Where new frames, new doors, mere deal, again and again have rotted.

Michael Hamburger

Oak Duir

June 10–July 7

I put my head in the bag of leaves
and breathed green. Coarse sourjuiced crushed
smell of wet summers, that sharp male taste;
foliate-faced I sucked green with each breath,
spaced out on oak. The fine drenching rain
felt seasidey. We walked the gleaming lane
that ribbons from hill to hill, slowly, dodging
odd Sunday cars, to our knees in tangled stalks,
flowering grasses, red cloverheads weighed down
with so much wet, the ditches murmuring.

Wine from oakleaves is tawny, tastes dark
and woody, midsummer evening fires, the sweet
smoke of peat. It is strong, climbs down deep
and blazes. It comes from the young growth;
the tender pink-flushed clusters of new leaf
offer themselves at a touch, break free
in showers of droplets, stalked green and sapped
like frankincense. You pour boiling water
on the stripped leaves: they smell of fresh tea.
The brew is bitter and brown; it could cure leather.

I sipped at last year's wine; thought, from now on
the nights draw in. The season's prime lay
stewed in a bin, filling our house with summer.
(I'm autumnal, best in receding light
in the dark half of the year.) Next day
I strained the stuff, added yeast and sweetness,
set the warm juice to work. Those clear green leaves
are bloodless now, bleached out: I have
their essence bottled up, breathed in, elixir of all
oaks in me, as the sun inches south.

Hilary Llewellyn-Williams
from Tree Calendar

'The oak inns creak in their joints as light declines'

The oak inns creak in their joints as light declines
from the ale-coloured skies of Warwickshire.
Autumn has blown the froth from the foaming orchards,
so white-haired regulars draw chairs nearer the grate
to spit on logs that crackle into leaves of fire.
But they grow deafer, not sure if what they hear
is the drone of the abbeys from matins to compline,
or the hornet's nest of a chain saw working late
on the knoll up there back of the Norman chapel.
Evening loosens the moth, the owl shifts its weight,

a fish-mouthed moon swims up from wavering elms,
but four old men are out on the garden benches,
talking of the bows they have drawn, their strings of wenches,
their coined eyes shrewdly glittering like the Thames'
estuaries. I heard their old talk carried
through cables laid across the Atlantic bed,
their gossip rustles like an apple orchard's
in my own head, and I can drop their names
like familiars—those bastard grandsires
whose maker granted them a primal pardon—
because the worm that cores the rotting apple
of the world and the hornet's chain saw cannot touch the words
of Shallow or Silence in their fading garden.

Derek Walcott

The Old Elm Tree by the River

Shrugging in the flight of its leaves,
it is dying. Death is slowly
standing up in its trunk and branches
like a camouflaged hunter. In the night
I am wakened by one of its branches
crashing down, heavy as a wall and then
lie sleepless, the world changed.
That is a life I know the country by.
Mine is a life I know the country by.
Willing to live and die, we stand here,
timely and at home, neighborly as two men.
Our place is changing in us as we stand,
and we hold up the weight that will bring us down.
In us the land enacts its history.
When we stood it was beneath us, and was
the strength by which we held to it
and stood, the daylight over it
a mighty blessing we cannot bear for long.

Wendell Berry

The Old Oak Tree

I sit beneath your leaves, old oak,
  You mighty one of all the trees;
Within whose hollow trunk a man
  Could stable his big horse with ease.

I see your knuckles hard and strong,
  But have no fear they'll come to blows;
Your life is long, and mine is short,
  But which has known the greater woes?

Thou hast not seen starved women here,
  Or man gone mad because ill-fed—
Who stares at stones in city streets,
  Mistaking them for hunks of bread.

Thou hast not felt the shivering backs
  Of homeless children lying down
And sleeping in the cold, night air—
  Like doors and walls, in London town.

Knowing thou hast not known such shame,
  And only storms have come thy way,
Methinks I could in comfort spend
  My summer with thee, day by day.

To lie by day in thy green shade,
  And in thy hollow rest at night;
And through the open doorway see
  The stars turn over leaves of light.

                              W. H. Davies

'Old Yew, which graspest at the stones'

Old Yew, which graspest at the stones
      That name the under-lying dead,
      Thy fibres net the dreamless head,
Thy roots are wrapt about the bones.

The seasons bring the flower again,
      And bring the firstling to the flock;
      And in the dusk of thee, the clock
Beats out the little lives of men.

O not for thee the glow, the bloom,
      Who changest not in any gale,
      Nor branding summer suns avail
To touch thy thousand years of gloom:

And gazing on thee, sullen tree,
      Sick for thy stubborn hardihood,
      I seem to fail from out my blood
And grow incorporate into thee.

Alfred, Lord Tennyson

On a Tree Fallen Across the Road
(To Hear Us Talk)

The tree the tempest with a crash of wood
Throws down in front of us is not to bar
Our passage to our journey's end for good,
But just to ask us who we think we are

Insisting always on our own way so.
She likes to halt us in our runner tracks,
And make us get down in a foot of snow
Debating what to do without an axe.

And yet she knows obstruction is in vain:
We will not be put off the final goal
We have it hidden in us to attain,
Not though we have to seize earth by the pole

And, tired of aimless circling in one place,
Steer straight off after something into space.

Robert Frost

Pine

Growing up under the weight of wardrobes,
we have awarded ourselves pine. The old veneers
have been stripped away. A Swedish wife welcomes us
with her frank stare and enlightened ideas.

White wood, bright wood, your blonde shavings
fall away like the curls of a pampered child.
My fingers drift across the grainy fingerprints,
the dusty contours, the tumuli and cliffs.

Only these knots hold me, like some feud
from the past—the bad migraines
mother used to get, or a ridge of low pressure
swishing its cloudbursts on the childhood fête.

But we will chamfer all that. When you called
this morning I was clearing our old dresser
of its tea-rings and nicks, the yellow sawdust
heaping up like salt-sift in a glass.

It's a walk through sand-dunes down to the sea,
the space where honesty might begin,
if we knew how, no corners to hide in,
the coming clean of our loyalties, and lies.

Blake Morrison

Pine-Trees and the Sky: Evening

I'd watched the sorrow of the evening sky,
And smelt the sea, and earth, and the warm clover,
And heard the waves, and the seagull's mocking cry.

And in them all was only the old cry,
That song they always sing—'The best is over!
You may remember now, and think, and sigh,
O silly lover!'
And I was tired and sick that all was over,
And because I,
For all my thinking, never could recover
One moment of the good hours that were over.
And I was sorry and sick, and wished to die.

Then from the sad west turning wearily,
I saw the pines against the white north sky,
Very beautiful, and still, and bending over
Their sharp black heads against a quiet sky.
And there was peace in them; and I
Was happy, and forgot to play the lover,
And laughed, and did no longer wish to die;
Being glad of you, O pine-trees and the sky!

Rupert Brooke
Lulworth, 8th July 1907

The Plantation

Any point in that wood
Was a centre, birch trunks
Ghosting your bearings,
Improvising charmed rings

Wherever you stopped.
Though you walked a straight line

It might be a circle you travelled
With toadstools and stumps

Always repeating themselves.
Or did you re-pass them?
Here were bleyberries quilting the floor,
The black char of a fire

And having found them once
You were sure to find them again.
Someone had always been there
Though always you were alone.

Lovers, birdwatchers,
Campers, gipsies and tramps
Left some trace of their trades
Or their excrement.

Hedging the road so
It invited all comers
To the hush and the mush
Of its whispering treadmill,

Its limits defined,
So they thought, from outside.
They must have been thankful
For the hum of the traffic

If they ventured in
Past the picnickers' belt
Or began to recall
Tales of fog on the mountains.

You had to come back
To learn how to lose yourself,
To be pilot and stray—witch,
Hansel and Gretel in one.

Seamus Heaney

Planting Trees

In the mating of trees,
the pollen grain entering invisible
the domed room of the winds, survives
the ghost of the old forest
that stood here when we came. The ground
invites it, and it will not be gone.
I become the familiar of that ghost
and its ally, carrying in a bucket
twenty trees smaller than weeds,
and I plant them along the way
of the departure of the ancient host.
I return to the ground its original music.
It will rise out of the horizon
of the grass, and over the heads
of the weeds, and it will rise over
the horizon of men's heads. As I age
in the world it will rise and spread,
and be for this place horizon
and orison, the voice of its winds.
I have made myself a dream to dream
of its rising, that has gentled my nights.
Let me desire and wish well the life
these trees may live when I
no longer rise in the mornings
to be pleased by the green of them
shining, and their shadows on the ground,
and the sound of the wind in them.

Wendell Berry

A Poison Tree

I was angry with my friend:
I told my wrath, my wrath did end.
I was angry with my foe:
I told it not, my wrath did grow.

And I water'd it in fears,
Night and morning with my tears;
And I sunned it with smiles,
And with soft deceitful wiles.

And it grew both day and night,
Till it bore an apple bright;
And my foe beheld it shine,
And he knew that it was mine,

And into my garden stole
When the night had veil'd the pole:
In the morning glad I see
My foe outstretch'd beneath the tree.

William Blake

The Poplar Field

The poplars are fell'd; farewell to the shade
And the whispering sound of the cool colonnade;
The winds play no longer and sing in the leaves,
Nor Ouse on his bosom their image receives.

Twelve years have elapsed since I first took a view
Of my favourite field and the bank where they grew:
And now in the grass behold they are laid,
And the tree is my seat that once lent me a shade.

The blackbird has fled to another retreat,
Where the hazels afford him a screen from the heat;
And the scene where his melody charm'd me before
Resounds with his sweet-flowing ditty no more.

My fugitive years are all hasting away,
And I must ere long lie as lowly as they,
With a turf on my breast and a stone at my head,
Ere another such grove shall arise in its stead.

'Tis a sight to engage me, if anything can,
To muse on the perishing pleasures of man;
Though his life be a dream, his enjoyments, I see,
Have a being less durable even than he.

William Cowper

Poplar Memory

I walked under the autumnal poplars that my father planted
On a day in April when I was a child
Running beside the heap of suckers
From which he picked the straightest, most promising,

My father dreamt forests, he is dead—
And there are poplar forests in the waste-places
And on the banks of drains.

When I look up
I see my father
Peering through the branched sky.

Patrick Kavanagh

Ronsard's Lament for the Cutting of the Forest of Gastine

Old forest, tall household of the birds, no more
Will nimble deer browse as they did before
Deep in your peaceful shade, and your green mane
No more will gentle summer's sun and rain.
No more will the amorous shepherd come to sit
Against a tree, his sheepdog at his feet,
To play upon his four-holed flute in praise
Of pretty Janet and her pleasing ways.
All will be mute, Echo be still for good.
There will be a field where your great trees stood,
Their airy shadows shifting in the light. Now
You will feel the coulter and the plow.
Your deep silence gone, breathless with fear,
Satyr and Pan will not again come here.
Farewell, old hall of the wind's high harmony,
Where I first made my lyre's tongues agree;
Where Calliope, so beautiful and good,
Gave me the love of her great sisterhood,
As if she cast a hundred roses over me;
Where Euterpe at her own breast nourished me.
Farewell, old trees, farewell, high sacred heads,
Once honored with rites and flowers, holy deeds,
Disdained by travellers now, your death their plight
Who burn in the summer sky's naked light—
Who, knowing no more your fresh green shade,
Curse your destroyers, wishing them destroyed.
Farewell, old oaks, once honoured by our creed
As fellow citizens, Dodonean seed,
Jupiter's trees, that first gave food to men,
Ungrateful men, who did not understand
Beneficence—a people utterly gross
To massacre these fathers who nourished us.
The man who trusts this world will not be free
Of grief. How true, O gods, is that philosophy

Which says that all things in the end will perish,
That by the deaths of forms new forms will flourish.
In time, a peak in Tempe's Vale will stand,
And Mount Athos will be a bottomland;
Neptune's fields, in time, will stand in grain.
All forms will pass, matter alone remain.

Wendell Berry

'Shut, too, in a tower of words, I mark'

. . . Shut, too, in a tower of words, I mark
On the horizon walking like the trees
The wordy shapes of women, and the rows
Of the star-gestured children in the park.
Some let me make you of the vowelled beeches,
Some of the oaken voices, from the roots
Of many a thorny shire tell you notes,
Some let me make you of the water's speeches . . .

Dylan Thomas
from Especially when the October Wind

The Silver Tree

In a hot steamed up room five girls are spinning
a tree made of silver paper, growing
from a trunk so clumsy only a child
could be taken in by it. Its girth outstrips
the attenuated branches that tumble
from its crown and drop down to the floor where
they coil and lengthen, lovelier than hair,

a genuine silver tree they seem to spin
out of themselves. Their fingers diminish,
twine with foil, are sucked out of their sleeves.
It is the triumph of Aluminium.

And just as they become the tree, the tree
becomes them. They thrive on ambiguity.
As the tree grows they grow, although
infinitely more slowly, and enter into
the frieze where mothers and smart daughters dance
in a cold pastoral. Ice is eating them.

It is desire for perpetuity,
the film rerunning as they petrify
and the forest throws its lank arms about them.
They hang like fruit, sucked out, perfect, until
imaginary gods pass by and cut them down.

George Szirtes

A Single Tree

You ask for more rungs in the ladder I
Built against the solitary tree:
Your legs still short, your brother up already.
So in wind I fix it, and I find
As I lean smoking, back against the tree,
Seagulls driving plovers from their ground,

A picture of two figures, both still young,
Who come across this ladder sagging, rotten,
Leant against a hedge-tree long forgotten,
And wonder at the nearness of each rung;
Watched by their father, trying not to long
To join them or wish again this day

Of wind and gulls and peewits fighting, crying,
Nostalgic falseness in the air, sighing sighing,
Though that was in his mind. So, today,
He takes two cold boys home and gives them food,
Glad he shared with them a single tree
Before they walked without him to the wood.

                                    P. J. Kavanagh

'The solemn work of building up the pyre'

. . . The solemn work of building up the pyre
Was done in splendour and they laid a fire
That reached to heaven in a cone of green.
The arms were twenty fathoms broad—I mean
The boughs and branches heaped upon the ground—
And straw in piles had first been loaded round.
    But how they made the funeral fires flame,
Or what the trees by number or by name
—Oak, fir-tree, birch, aspen and poplar too,
Ilex and alder, willow, elm and yew,
Box, chestnut, plane, ash, laurel, thorn and lime,
Beech, hazel, whipple-tree—I lack the time
To tell you, or who felled them, nor can tell
How their poor gods ran up and down the dell
All disinherited of habitation,
Robbed of their quiet and in desolation,
The nymph and dryad of the forest lawn,
The hamadryad and the subtle faun,
These I pass over, birds and beasts as well
That fled in terror when the forest fell,
Nor shall I say how in the sudden light
Of the unwonted sun the dell took fright,
Nor how the fire first was couched in straw,
Then in dry sticks thrice severed with a saw,
Then in green wood with spice among the stems
And then in cloth-of-gold with precious gems

And many a flower-garland in the stir
Of breathing incense and the scent of myrrh;
Nor how Arcita lay among it all,
Nor of the wealth and splendour of his pall
Nor yet how Emily thrust in the fire
As custom was and lit the funeral pyre . . .

Geoffrey Chaucer
from The Knight's Tale

Some Trees

These are amazing: each
Joining a neighbor, as though speech
Were a still performance.
Arranging by chance

To meet as far this morning
From the world as agreeing
With it, you and I
Are suddenly what the trees try

To tell us we are:
That their merely being there
Means something; that soon
We may touch, love, explain.

And glad not to have invented
Such comeliness, we are surrounded:
A silence already filled with noises,
A canvas on which emerges

A chorus of smiles, a winter morning.
Placed in a puzzling fight, and moving,
Our days put on such reticence
These accents seem their own defense.

John Ashbery

Song of the Open Road

I think that I shall never see
A billboard lovely as a tree.
Indeed, unless the billboards fall
I'll never see a tree at all.

Ogden Nash

Song of the Stand-pipe

Look the trees are dying in the drought
beech and birch keel over
shallow roots clutch at crumbling earth
copper and silver become uncurrent
beaten too soon into autumn
yet the leaden plane
sheds again
its patched hide
with seventeenth century resilience
whatever civil war
the elements embark on
sun against rain
it stands
making its rough balls to propagate
citizen not recorded in the wild state
hybrid
tough cockney
that will uproot the paving stones
if we should ever
decamp
and lace its branches beautifully
over the crumpled streets.
When elm and oak
are bugged and broken
like love it will be here
nave and aisles

when the next first men
come wondering back
into the tumbled city
to begin again.

Maureen Duffy

South Wind

Where have you been, South Wind, this May-day
    morning,—
With larks aloft, or skimming with the swallow,
Or with blackbirds in a green, sun-glinted thicket?

Oh, I heard you like a tyrant in the valley;
Your ruffian haste shook the young, blossoming orchards;
You clapped rude hands, hallooing round the chimney,
And white your pennons streamed along the river.

You have robbed the bee, South Wind, in your adventure,
Blustering with gentle flowers; but I forgave you
When you stole to me shyly with scent of hawthorn.

Siegfried Sassoon

Stovewood

two thousand years of fog and sucking minerals
    from the soil,
Russian river ox-team & small black train
    haul to mill;
fresh-sawed rough cut by wagon
    and built into a barn;
tear it down and split it up
    and stick it in a stove.

Gary Snyder

'Survivor sole, and hardly such, of all'

Survivor sole, and hardly such, of all
That once liv'd here thy brethren, at my birth
(Since which I number three-score winters past)
A shatter'd veteran, hollow-trunk'd perhaps
As now, and with excoriate forks deform,
Relicts of ages! Could a mind, imbued
With truth from heav'n, created thing adore,
I might with rev'rence kneel and worship thee.
        It seems idolatry with some excuse
When our forefather Druids in their oaks
Imagin'd sanctity. The conscience yet
Unpurified by an authentic act
Of amnesty, the meed of blood divine,
Lov'd not the light, but gloomy into gloom
Of thickest shades, like Adam after taste
Of fruit proscrib'd, as to a refuge, fled.
        Thou wast a bauble once; a cup and ball,
Which babes might play with; and the thievish jay
Seeking her food, with ease might have purloin'd
The auburn nut that held thee, swallowing down
Thy yet close-folded latitude of boughs
And all thine embryo vastness, at a gulp.
But Fate thy growth decreed: autumnal rains
Beneath thy parent tree mellow'd the soil
Design'd thy cradle, and a skipping deer,
With pointed hoof dibbling the glebe, prepar'd
The soft receptacle in which secure
Thy rudiments should sleep the winter through.
        So Fancy dreams—Disprove it, if ye can,
Ye reas'ners broad awake, whose busy search
Of argument, employ'd too oft amiss,
Sifts half the pleasures of short life away.
        Thou fell'st mature, and in the loamy clod
Swelling, with vegetative force instinct
Didst burst thine egg, as theirs the fabled Twins,
Now stars; two lobes, protruding, pair'd exact:

A leaf succeeded, and another leaf,
And all the elements thy puny growth
Fost'ring propitious, thou becam'st a twig.
    Who liv'd when thou wast such? Oh couldst thou speak,
As in Dodona once thy kindred trees
Oracular, I would not curious ask
The future, best unknown, but at thy mouth
Inquisitive, the less ambiguous past.
    By thee I might correct, erroneous oft,
The clock of history, facts and events
Timing more punctual, unrecorded facts
Recov'ring, and misstated setting right—
Desp'rate attempt, till trees shall speak again!
    Time made thee what thou wast—King of the woods;
And time hath made thee what thou art—a cave
For owls to roost in. Once thy spreading boughs
O'erhung the champain; and the numerous flock
That graz'd it stood beneath that ample cope
Uncrowded yet safe-shelter'd from the storm.
No flock frequents thee now. Thou hast outliv'd
Thy popularity and art become
(Unless verse rescue thee awhile) a thing
Forgotten, as the foliage of thy youth.
    While thus through all the stages thou hast push'd
Of treeship, first a seedling hid in grass,
Then twig, then sapling, and, as century roll'd
Slow after century, a giant bulk
Of girth enormous, with moss-cushioned root
Upheav'd above the soil, and sides imboss'd
With prominent wens globose, till at the last
The rottenness, which Time is charg'd t' inflict
On other mighty ones, found also thee—
What exhibitions various hath the world
Witness'd of mutability in all
That we account most durable below!
Change is the diet, on which all subsist
Created changeable, and change at last

Destroys them.—Skies uncertain now the heat
Transmitting cloudless, and the solar beam
Now quenching in a boundless sea of clouds,—
Calm and alternate storm, moisture and drought,
Invigorate by turns the springs of life
In all that live, plant, animal, and man,
And in conclusion mar them. Nature's threads,
Fine passing thought, ev'n in her coarsest works,
Delight in agitation, yet sustain
The force that agitates, not unimpaired,
But, worn by frequent impulse, to the cause
Of their best tone their dissolution owe.
      Thought cannot spend itself, comparing still
The great and little of thy lot, thy growth
From almost nullity into a state
Of matchless grandeur, and declension thence
Slow into such magnificent decay.
Time was, when, settling on thy leaf, a fly
Could shake thee to the root—and time has been
When tempests could not. At thy firmest age
Thou hadst within thy bole solid contents
That might have ribb'd the sides or plank'd the deck
Of some flagg'd admiral; and tortuous arms,
The ship-wright's darling treasure, didst present
To the four-quarter'd winds, robust and bold,
Warp'd into tough knee-timber, many a load.
But the axe spar'd thee; in those thriftier days
Oaks fell not, hewn by thousands, to supply
The bottomless demands of contest wag'd
For senatorial honours. Thus to Time
The task was left to whittle thee away
With his sly scythe, whose ever-nibbling edge
Noiseless, an atom and an atom more
Disjoining from the rest, has, unobserv'd,
Achiev'd a labour, which had, far and wide,
(By man perform'd) made all the forest ring . . .

William Cowper
from Yardley Oak

The Tables Turned

Up! up! my friend, and clear your looks,
Why all this toil and trouble?
Up! up! my friend, and quit your books,
Or surely you'll grow double.

The sun above the mountain's head,
A freshening lustre mellow,
Through all the long green fields has spread,
His first sweet evening yellow.

Books! 'tis a dull and endless strife,
Come, hear the woodland linnet,
How sweet his music; on my life
There's more of wisdom in it.

And hark! how blithe the throstle sings!
And he is no mean preacher;
Come forth into the light of things
Let Nature be your teacher.

She has a world of ready wealth,
Our minds and hearts to bless—
Spontaneous wisdom breathed by health,
Truth breathed by chearfulness.

One impulse from a vernal wood
May teach you more of man;
Of moral evil and of good,
Than all the sages can.

Sweet is the lore which nature brings;
Our meddling intellect
Misshapes the beauteous forms of things;—
—We murder to dissect.

Enough of science and of art;
Close up these barren leaves;
Come forth, and bring with you a heart
That watches and receives.

William Wordsworth

The Tall Fruit-Trees

I'll lop them, it will be easier so to tend them;
  Then we may clean them, and gather the fruit with ease;
  No one can do with these great old orchard trees,
Dirty, shady, unwieldy—don't try to defend them.

O promise to do them one or two at a time then—
  That will make you twenty years in going the rounds:
Then the tall tops for me will be out of bounds,
  Surely I shall no longer be able to climb then.

But while I am able O let me ascend the plum-tree
  And poke my head out at the top, where the lovely view
Has a foreground of scarlet plums with a wash of blue,
  And I am away from earth in the starling's country.

And for a few years yet spend a day in the pear-tree,
  Squirming and stretching, plagued by the wasps and the twigs,
Scratches all over me, bruised in the arms and legs,
  Coming down whacked at last from the great old bare tree—

And yet not wholly bare, for his topmost steeple
  Still flaunts a fair wreath of a dozen, the best of all;
Ha, he beat me at last, for he was so tall—
  He will not give his best work up to greedy people.

And there is the huge gaunt apple-tree, dead man's seedling,
    With five great limbs, spreading twenty feet from the ground;
How he makes us stagger the longest ladder around,
    So heavy—yet four feet short of the ladder we're needing.

Some years he's good for bushels of small red apples
    That keep well enough, and roast well enough by the fire,
But every year he is young and brave with desire,
    Smothered in rosy wreaths that the sunlight dapples.

Dappled with sunlight and bright with the May-time raindrop,
    Mighty from age and youthful with tender bloom,
He heaves up brightness and scent to our highest room,
    Brushes the dormer-window with shining maintop.

We'll take in a bit more ground, and plant it with limber
    Maidens on dwarfing stocks, at twelve feet apart;
But the great old trees are the real loves of my heart,
    Mountains of blossom and fruit on the stalwart timber.

Ruth Pitter

'There grew a goodly tree him faire beside'

There grew a goodly tree him faire beside,
    Loaden with fruit and apples rosie red,
    As they in pure vermilion had beene dide,
    Whereof great vertues ouer all were red:
    For happie life to all, which thereon fed,
    And life eke euerlasting did befall:
    Great God it planted in that blessed sted
    With his almightie hand, and did it call
The tree of life, the crime of our first fathers fall.

In all the world like was not to be found,
  Saue in that soile, where all good things did grow,
  And freely sprong out of the fruitfull ground,
  As incorrupted Nature did them sow,
  Till that dread Dragon all did ouerthrow.
  Another like faire tree eke grew thereby,
  Whereof who so did eat, eftsoones did know
  Both good and ill: O mornefull memory:
That tree through one mans fault hath doen vs all to dy.

Edmund Spenser
from The Faerie Queene

'There is an old tale goes that Herne the Hunter'

Mrs Page: There is an old tale goes that Herne the Hunter,
Sometime a keeper here in Windsor Forest,
Doth all the winter-time, at still midnight,
Walk round about an oak, with great ragg'd horns;
And there he blasts the tree, and takes the cattle,
And makes milche-kine yield blood, and shakes a chain
In a most hideous and dreadful manner.
You have heard of such a spirit, and well you know
The superstitious idle-headed eld
Receiv'd, and did deliver to our age,
This tale of Herne the Hunter for a truth.
  Page: Why yet there want not many that do fear
In deep of night to walk by this Herne's oak.
But what of this?
  Mrs Ford: Marry, this is our device—
That Falstaff at that oak shall meet with us,
Disguis'd, like Herne, with huge horns on his head.

William Shakespeare
from The Merry Wives of Windsor

'There is a thorn; it looks so old'

There is a thorn; it looks so old,
In truth you'd find it hard to say,
How it could ever have been young,
It looks so old and grey.
Not higher than a two-years' child,
It stands erect this aged thorn;
No leaves it has, no thorny points;
It is a mass of knotted joints,
A wretched thing forlorn.
It stands erect, and like a stone
With lichens it is overgrown.

Like rock or stone, it is o'ergrown
With lichens to the very top,
And hung with heavy tufts of moss,
A melancholy crop:
Up from the earth these mosses creep,
And this poor thorn they clasp it round
So close, you'd say that they were bent
With plain and manifest intent,
To drag it to the ground;
And all had joined in one endeavour
To bury this poor thorn for ever . . .

William Wordsworth
from The Thorn

'There was an old lady whose folly'

There was an old lady whose folly,
Induced her to sit in a holly:
Wherefrom by a thorn, her gown being torn,
She quickly become melancholly.

Edward Lear

'There was an old man in a tree'

There was an old man in a tree,
Whose whiskers were lovely to see;
But the birds of the air, pluck'd them perfectly bare,
To make themselves nests in that tree.

Edward Lear

The Thicket

I

My weald of tales, my beech leaves, my bronze.
A world of trees shades the land's shadow.
Under the tribe's winter, roots of iron,

Roots of grain; and at the thicket's heart
A man's tread, a bird-cry, the glitter
Of a pool rippled with a stone blade,

His last gift. My green eye shuts. Slowly
Drops of light in the night sky falter
My gifts for him: The Hunter, the Plough.

II

Through the trees, through the ferns, through the dark:
A blade shrived with the eyes of a beast
And its five wounds. Armour chafes the spell

Of the wood, my runes, my tree-letters
Mumble in stones. Deeper the heart folds
Leaves about the rood's axe-shaft, a grove

Where the scaled Worm, the Ravager, lurks.
Through my paths, through my thorns, through my tale
The earl's bard tracks him and will not err.

III

The duke's forest domain. Here his verge
Of grant harbours in their old fastness
His loyal-made beasts, the boar, the stag,

The archers' spoils; now they divide them
And sojourn here in the branched covert.
Manor and parlance, the haunch is theirs.

Faint carols of the horn—young Roland
Quartered in the blood of Harold—chase
Home to the toils a mort for Rufus.

IV

I heard this ballad in the green wood
Where the king's deer rustle in the brake
And it ransomed my heart merrily.

A man's face peers from the tangled oaks,
Arrows bristle in the poor slain deer,
An antlered head grinning like a man.

The song curls out from the forest edge,
Where rooks drop to the castle tower,
And the wood-doves call, Law, Law, Outlaw.

V

The land till dusk. Limbs of a torn elm
Lapse in thin blue smoke. Your kindled hearth
Fades in the dome of the common-weal:

A man gathering a few dry sticks,
Masters who gather fields together.
From hedgerow and ditch of a new world

The ship of state, keeled with oak, lunges
Into the western beam, where poor Jack
Harrows hell in the Virginia woods.

VI

Eyes of fire peering from the forest—
I heard the hammering of iron
Where the hidden streams are dammed in ponds.

I looked for you, your bundles of sticks,
Hazel, chestnut, hurdles, poles for hops:
Fence-posts and the forbidden hedge-rows.

I walked further up the mill-valley.
Charcoal and white-heat have bleared my hands.
Darker smoke than these comes down the line.

VII

There the lawn slopes out into the grain.
Close to the house, walks of fir and ash
Screen the chaste delights of company.

Art extends the long wooded vista
Where sense and taste dapple in the shade,
As a path winds through the tidy grove

To the home of the god Silvanus.
Here my lord may peruse in autumn
The green margin of Rome's dead pages.

VIIII

A life of the woods. The oak and elm
The beech and the fir, fell to my axe,
To be cut to shape in the ship-yard.

So a ship took me and death met me
Where the sound living in the dead wood
Is drowned in the green heart of the waves.

Weaker than the beams I took work from,
Among spars and splinters of the fleet,
My head nods towards a bare foreland.

IX

Dark places of a year uncommon,
Felled trunks bright red with speckles of rot,
Shapes of leaves moving over the heath.

I stumbled here. Failure, self-grandeur
Harvest the swollen grain. My ruin
Of the farm swarms with ivy, owl-hoots.

Here I hang. The shrill tongues of rick-fires
Light home my fellow good Captain Swing,
Scrawl our names on a roll of thunder.

X

Dull weight of the bird with bright feathers.
The dark wood casts its net over us.
My lord's men and the dead moon are out.

A fox hounded into the green web.
Horsemen are out, swathes of trees are down,
Field-men caught by vermin in a snare

Where the hares caper under the law.
All the wild ones running in the wood
Dance to my tune, at my belt, tonight.

XI

Mourning and mourning for the lost woods
My lord's debts have felled, the dear thicket
Where small creatures lived, lost to the plough,

The land I looked for was innocence.
Solitary in the fields I watched
A world furious and imperfect

Drawing clear from the melancholy
Of a shrouded elm in a thorn hedge—
A beauty I could not understand.

XII

Ghosts of the world-wood: the trees are felled,
Stumps; puny saplings which replace them
Will outgrow me and then outlive me.

Feeble traceries of twigs, the past
Thrusts from the black mould of the present.
There is a deep thicket to move through,

Tangles, smarts, and patches of soft grass,
Disease and drought, till the trees are felled
And bare ground grows a little clearer.

Michael Vince

'This night I walk through a forest in my head'

This night I walk through a forest in my head;
    In each tree's heart a lute, waiting the skill
    Of hand to chisel it, is musical,
    Already with a song stirring the glade;

All the hard wood cries to the stars that float
    Among the leaves, bird-sweet and shrill,
    Though no wires stretch nor delicate fingers mete
    Out their divisions, nor lute-master's skill.

And so, bewildered like one newly dead
    Who finds the myrtle-groves of Hades strange
    Country to him, I go among the trees

Seeking your image flickering through the shade,
    A madman's fire, and thus deluded range
    Cold hollows of my skull and echoing silences.

John Heath-Stubbs

'Thrise happie hee, who by some shadie Grove'

Thrise happie hee, who by some shadie Grove
Farre from the clamorous World doth live his owne,
Though solitarie, yet who is not alone,
But doth converse with that *Eternall Love.*
O how more sweet is Birds harmonious Mone,
Or the soft Sobbings of the widow'd Dove?
Than those smoothe Whisp'rings neare a Princes Throne,
Which Good make doubtfull, doe the Evill approve.
O how more sweet is *Zephyres* wholesome Breath,
And Sighs perfum'd, which doe the Flowres unfold,

Than that Applause vaine *Honour* doth bequeath?
How sweete are Streames to Poyson drunke in Gold?
The World is full of Horrours, Falshoods, Slights,
Woods silent Shades have only true Delights.

William Drummond

Throwing a Tree
New Forest

The two executioners stalk along over the knolls,
Bearing two axes with heavy heads shining and wide,
And a long limp two-handled saw toothed for cutting great boles,
And so they approach the proud tree that bears the death-mark on
its side.

Jackets doffed they swing axes and chop away just above ground,
And the chips fly about and lie white on the moss and fallen
leaves;
Till a broad deep gash in the bark is hewn all the way round,
And one of them tries to hook upward a rope, which at last he
achieves.

The saw then begins, till the top of the tall giant shivers:
The shivers are seen to grow greater each cut than before:
They edge out the saw, tug the rope; but the tree only quivers,
And kneeling and sawing again, they step back and try pulling once
more.

Then, lastly, the living mast sways, further sways: with a shout
Job and Ike rush aside. Reached the end of its long staying
powers
The tree crashes downward: it shakes all its neighbours
throughout,
And two hundred years' steady growth has been ended in less than
two hours.

Thomas Hardy

Timber

In the avenues of yesterday
A tree might have a thing to say.
    Horsemen then heard
    From the branches a word
That sent them serious on their way.

A tree, —a beam, a box, a crutch,
Costing so little or so much;
    Wainscot or stair,
    Barge, baby's chair,
A pier, a flute, a mill, a hutch.

That tree uprooted lying there
Will make such things with knack and care,
    Unless you hear
    From its boughs too clear
The word that has whitened the traveller's hair.

                    Edmund Blunden

To a Late Poplar

Not yet half-drest
O tardy bride!
And the priest
And the bridegroom and the guests
Have been waiting a full hour.

The meadow choir
Is playing the wedding march
Two fields away,
And squirrels are already leaping in ecstasy
Among leaf-full branches.

                    Patrick Kavanagh

To a Tree in London
(Clement's Inn)

Here you stay
Night and day,
Never, never going away!

Do you ache
When we take
Holiday for our health's sake?

Wish for feet
When the heat
Scalds you in the brick-built street,

That you might
Climb the height
Where your ancestry saw light,

Find a brook
In some nook
There to purge your swarthy look?

No. You read
Trees to need
Smoke like earth whereon to feed . . .

Have no sense
That far hence
Air is sweet in a blue immense,

Thus, black, blind,
You have opined
Nothing of your brightest kind;

Never seen
Miles of green,
Smelt the landscape's sweet serene.

Thomas Hardy

To Make a Tree

Take wood, seasoned or green,
    rough-hewn or planed.
Take first one four-square beam
    twice a man's height,
then graft a second, half that,
    on to it
cross-wise and near the top,
    cunningly joined.
Dig socket. Plant upright.
    Hope it will root,
hope sap will rise. If not,
    keep tools at hand
and, when the time is ripe,
    nail up the fruit.

Paul Hyland

Tree

Grotesquely shaped, this stubbed tree craves a madman's
    eye,
its convoluted pipes lie tortured on the air,
twist black, turn back to fanged twigs and attitudes,
its dusty leaves quite stunted, still it will not die.

In rousing spring its frugal green was last to bud,
in autumn will be the first to anticipate the fall.
Now, aimlessly, I give it human attributes:
its mud-coloured bark, sick flesh; sap, a victim's blood.

As, sometimes, a child, contorting his plastic face
to make another laugh, is told to cease his play
lest abstract fate solidifies both lips and eyes,
horrifically, to one perpetual grimace;

so, perhaps, this maimed structure postured once and
      thus—
a buffoon amidst these oaks. Then laughter shook
untimely leaves down till avenging lightning struck,
petrified the attitude, a spectacle for us.

August—other trees conform, are properly dressed;
but this funny one exists for funny children,
easy to climb, easy to insult, or throw stones at,
and only urgent lovers in its shade will rest.

Yet this pauper, this caliban tree, let good men praise,
for it survives, and that's enough; more, on gala nights,
with copper beech and silver birch it too can soar
unanchored, free, in prosperous moonlight and amaze.

Dannie Abse

A Tree

Under unending interrogation by wind
Tortured by huge scaldings of light
Tries to confess all but could not
Bleed a word

Stripped to its root letter, cruciform
Contorted
Tried to tell all

Through crooking of elbows
Twitching of finger-ends.

Finally
Resigned
To be dumb.

Lets what happens to it happen.

Ted Hughes

The Tree

I stood still and was a tree amid the wood,
Knowing the truth of things unseen before;
Of Daphne and the laurel bow
And that god-feasting couple old
That grew elm-oak amid the wold.
'Twas not until the gods had been
Kindly entreated, and been brought within
Unto the hearth of their heart's home
That they might do this wonder thing;
Nathless I have been a tree amid the wood
And many a new thing understood
That was rank folly to my head before.

Ezra Pound

The Tree

This child, shovelling away
what remains of snow—
a batter of ash and crystals—
knows nothing of the pattern
his bent back lifts
above his own reflection:
it climbs the street-lamp's stem
and cross-bar, branching
to take in all the lines
from gutter, gable, slates
and chimney-crowns to the high
pillar of a mill chimney
on a colourless damp sky:
there in its topmost air
and eyrie rears that tree

his bending sends up
from a treeless street, its roots
in the eye and in the net the shining
flagstones spread at his feet.

Charles Tomlinson

The Tree

Tree, lend me this root,
That I may sit here at your foot
And watch these hawking flies that wheel
And perch on the air's hand
And red-thighed bees
That fan the dust with their wings' breeze.
Do you not feel me on your heel,
My bone against your bone?
Or are you in such slumber sunk,
Woodpeckers knocking at your trunk
Find you are not at home?
To winds you are not dumb;
Then tell me, if you understand:
When your thick timber has been hewn,
Its boards in floors and fences sewn,
And you no more a tree,
Where will your dryad be?

Andrew Young

Tree Fall

The saw rasps the morning into logs
that chart a tree's slow foundering
sinking to a barky knee, a marooned stump
island in the woven green lawn.
Its head of mermaid hair drops, jerks on a hangman rope

its spread arms own gallows fork the clear sky
where the young executioner swings Tarzan
though the urban jungle, silhouetted
in stark bravado every window fills
to watch, admire up there mid-July
half naked in a sudden sunburst
as the top bows to his overgrown powerdrill
we tame at home to trim the prunus
that burgeons white hopes in the Spring.
Blinded by sun moths stagger drunk with sleep
from their doomed leaf beds. Silent in the ripped air
predator thrush and blackbird let them go.
This was a false acacia, immigrant
a locust tree, John Baptist fed on
with honey for desert breakfast, native
from the New World three hundred years ago.
The tree fellers prise its spread fingers
from their grip on the earth.
I take up a slice of trunk fallen to the ground
its sunshield kept bare of other life
as the ash drips its poison onto the soil
at its feet, an invisible wall
that moats and guards it round.
My slice shows annuities: late spring, drought, flood
mapped in its rings, graphed so fine my naked eye
can't tell them round. Maybe this morning
has shipwrecked two centuries and Mozart
is playing at the inmost ring. From Cologne bridge
you can see beyond mythical Christpoint
back to when we were children of the wood spirits
and knew what we did when we cut down trees.
See that ringed jetty? Its timbers plot
where the ships tied up with oil, gods
wine, cooking pots, the centuries before the axe.
I hold an ache, oak corn in my palm.
The earth will make it a chronometer
and I can only guess at the time it will
tick over when the lasersaw brings it down.

Maureen Duffy

The Tree in the Goods Yard

So sigh, that hearkening pasts arouse
In the magic circle of your boughs,—
So timelessly, on sound's deep sea,
Sail your unfurled melody,
             My small dark Tree.

Who set you in this smoky yard
None tells me; it might seem too hard
A fate for a tree whose place should be
With a sounding proud-plumed company
             By a glittering sea.

And yet you live with liking here,
Are well, have some brocade to wear,
And solitary, mysteriously
Revoice light airs as sighs, which free
             Tombed worlds for me.

Edmund Blunden

Tree-kill

Chip chop
Chip chop
Down comes a tree

Chip chop
Wallop plop
Help, its fallen on me!

Chip chop
Chip chop
Down comes another

Chip chop
Wheee! bop!
That one fell on mother

Chip chop
Chip chop
Crush on daddys head!

Chip chop
Please stop
Or else we'll *all* be dead!

Spike Milligan

The Tree of Guilt

When first we knew it, gibbet-bare
It scrawled an omen on the air,
But later, in its wealth of leaf,
Looked too lush to hang a thief;

And from its branches muffled doves
Drummed out the purchasable loves
Which far below them were purveyed
On credit through the slinking shade.

And what a cooing trade was done
Around that tree-trunk anyone
Could guess who saw the countless hearts
Carved in its bark transfixed with darts;

So entering this enchanted zone
Anyone would add his own
Cut neatly with a pocket knife,
There for his life and the tree's life.

And having thus signed on the line
Anyone claimed his anodyne
And, drinking it, was lulled asleep
By doves and insects, deep and deep,

Till he finds later, waking cold,
The leaves fallen, himself old,
And his carved heart, though vastly grown,
Not recognizably his own.

The dove's is now the raven's day
And there is interest yet to pay;
And in those branches, gibbet-bare,
Is that a noose that dangles there?

Louis MacNeice

Tree of Heaven

Harvard has famous elms, Boston its maples,
Somerville, weeds.
Nothing thrives on the city's neglect like ailanthus.
It fattens, and breeds.
While oaks, beeches—Massachusetts natives—
Shrink back, poisoned by the Interstate,
Stinking ailanthus feeds
On the pear-drop scent of car body-shops,
The green oil-slick on the pavement:
Immigrant trees.

They are everywhere: at the roots of supermarkets;
They attack
Garbage skips, parking lots, doorways of seedy
Italian restaurants, creeping surreptitiously:
Buckle and crack
The backs of the sidewalks, bursting skywards

To glimpse the blue Boston roofline through the fumes.
On the rank railroad tracks
They stitch up the left behind push-carts and milk-crates,
Undoing the past.

Soon bolted gable-high, they don't age well; their branches snap,
The cheap sticks split.
One strong wind can tear ailanthus' roots right out
And skittle it.
Seeding furtively behind the peeling porches, musty, dark
Back rooms of funeral homes and junk-shops, sloughing samaras,
They seem the opposite
Of a tree's true, permanent embodiment of place. And yet,
Though they're ephemeral you can't get rid of them; they are
Wholly appropriate.

Ineradicable Heaven Tree: feather-leaves fanning
The stifling yard,
Where an old man sits cursing its stragglers that sap
The statue of Mary among his tomatoes,
It wheedles its hard
Suckers through shallow dust; drops hayfever flowers,
A litter of rusty keys; and nothing about it
Is lovely, apart
From its name and its green shoots, mending the damage
It springs from, like scars.

Katrina Porteous

Tree Party

Your health, Master Willow. Contrive me a bat
To strike a red ball; apart from that
In the last resort I must hang my harp on you.

Your health, Master Oak. You emblem of strength,
Why must your doings be done at such length?
Beware lest the ironclad ages catch up with you.

Your health, Master Blackthorn. Be live and be quick,
Provide the black priest with a big black stick
That his ignorant flock may go straight for the fear of you.

Your health, Master Palm. If you brew us some toddy
To deliver us out of by means of the body,
We will burn all our bridges and rickshaws in praise of you.

Your health, Master Pine. Though sailing be past
Let you fly your own colours upon your own mast
And rig us a crow's nest to keep a look out from you.

Your health, Master Elm. Of giants arboreal
Poets have found you the most immemorial
And yet the big winds may discover the fault in you.

Your health, Master Hazel. On Hallow-e'en
Your nuts are to gather but not to be seen
Are the twittering ghosts that perforce are alive in you.

Your health, Master Holly. Of all the trees
That decorate parlour walls you please
Yet who would have thought you had so much blood in you?

Your health, Master Apple. Your topmost bough
Entices us to come climbing now
For all that old rumour there might be a snake in you.

Your health, Master Redwood. The record is yours
For the girth that astounds, the sap that endures,
But where are the creatures that once came to nest in you?

Your health, Master Banyan, but do not get drunk
Or you may not distinguish your limbs from your trunk
And the sense of Above and Below will be lost on you.

Your health, Master Bo-Tree. If Buddha should come
Yet again, yet again make your branches keep mum
That his words yet again may drop honey by leave of you.

Your health, Master Yew. My bones are few
And I fully admit my rent is due,
But do not be vexed, I will postdate a cheque for you.

Louis MacNeice

Trees

Trees, our mute companions,
looming through the winter mist
from the side of the road,
lit for a moment in passing
by the car's headlamps:
ash and oak, chestnut and yew;
witnesses, huge mild beings
who suffer the consequence
of sharing our planet and cannot
move away from any evil
we subject them to,
whose silent absolution hides
the scars of our sins, who always
forgive—yet still assume
the attributes of judges, not victims.

Ruth Fainlight

The Trees

The trees are coming into leaf
Like something almost being said;
The recent buds relax and spread,
Their greenness is a kind of grief.

Is it that they are born again
And we grow old? No, they die too.

Their yearly trick of looking new
Is written down in rings of grain.

Yet still the unresting castles thresh
In fullgrown thickness every May.
Last year is dead, they seem to say,
Begin afresh, afresh, afresh.

Philip Larkin

Trees Be Company

When zummer's burnen het's a-shed
Upon the droopen grasses head,
A-drevèn under sheädy leaves
The workvo'k in their snow-white sleeves,
We then mid yearn to clim' the height,
    Where thorns be white, above the vern;
An' aïr do turn the zunsheen's might
    To softer light too weak to burn—
      On woodless downs we mid be free,
      But lowland trees be company.

Though downs mid show a wider view
O' green a-reachen into blue
Than roads a-winden in the glen,
An' ringen wi' the sounds o' men;
The thissle's crown o' red an' blue
    In Fall's cwold dew do wither brown,
An' larks come down 'ithin the lew,
    As storms do brew, an' skies do frown—
      An' though the down do let us free,
      The lowland trees be company.

Where birds do zing, below the zun,
In trees above the blue-smok'd tun,
An' sheädes o' stems do overstratch
The mossy path 'ithin the hatch;
If leaves be bright up over head,
    When Maÿ do shed its glitt'ren light;
Or, in the blight o'Fall do spread
    A yollow bed avore our zight—
        Whatever season it mid be,
        The trees be always company.

When dusky night do nearly hide
The path along the hedge's zide,
An' daylight's hwomely sounds be still
But sounds o'water at the mill;
Then if noo feäce we long'd to greet
    Could come to meet our lwonesome treäce;
Or if noo peäce o'weary veet,
    However fleet, could reach its pleäce—
        However lwonesome we mid be,
        The trees would still be company.

William Barnes

Trees in a Town

Why must they fell two chestnuts on the road?
I did not see the lorry and its load
Before a wall had grown where they had stood,
I wish I thought that sphinxlike block was good
Builders have raised, to brood upon the loss
Of those two chestnuts where the two roads cross.
In spite of all the gain some say has been,
How can my eyes accept the altered scene?
How often, checked here on my way to work
By the instant luck of life, I saw themes fork

Into the boughs, where thought could learn as much
As sight will learn, till it is taught by touch.
In March abounding sunlight drenched the tree,
But still those sticky buds would not set free
Their secret fledgling silk of crumpled fronds
Held in the icy trance of winter's bonds.
Summer's wide green brought gloom where eyes could range
Up the dark foliage of attentive change;
But soon that gloom was battered by a squall,
Then the long, yellow leaves were first to fall.

After, in a frost, when all the boughs were bare,
What sudden grace the trees would print on air.
Call either tree a book for men to read
In any season; and then ask what need
A foursquare building had to pull them down.
I can forgive the traffic of this town
Its noise and brutal speed, but only just.
Metal and brick and glass above the dust
Smile on the road and on the lawn between
What else is there the planners have not seen?
A fig-tree, thick with fruit which never grows
Ripe in our sun. When June is here it throws
Young, yellow fruit to the pavement while, unspent,
The broad leaves thrive and spread a fertile scent,
Warm memory of abundant nature's loins.
The shrivelled figs grow hard as ringing coins,
Seeming to prove the toll-gate has been paid
Out of that garden to the builder's trade.
How patient is the shadow those leaves cast:
They rob the Present who despoil the Past;
In all Utility's cold eye has seen
Beauty's profusion yields to what is mean,
And yet a fallen leaf can still express
Man's exile, his lost innocence, his dress.

Trees in a town, how long will they survive
The merchant's axe for all that looks alive?
How shall miraculous blossom, leaf and seed
Breathe life into the body lulled by speed,
Racing to nothing in an asphalt place?
Something is lost. The trees' obstructive grace
Seems to slick progress wasteful and obscene,
Whose highway must be useful and be clean.

Vernon Watkins

The Trees in Tubs

Little laurel trees, your roots can find
No mountain, yet your leaves extend
Beyond your own world, into mine
Perennial wands, unfolding in my thought
The budding evergreen of time.

Kathleen Raine

A Tree Song

Of all the trees that grow so fair,
        Old England to adorn,
Greater are none beneath the Sun
        Than Oak, and Ash, and Thorn.
Sing Oak, and Ash and Thorn, good sirs,
        (All of a Midsummer morn!)
Surely we sing no little thing
        In Oak, and Ash, and Thorn!

Oak of Clay lived many a day
        Or ever Æneas began.
Ash of the Loam was a lady at home
        When Brut was an outlaw man.

Thorn of the Down saw New Troy Town
    (From which was London born);
Witness hereby the ancientry
    Of Oak, and Ash, and Thorn!

Yew that is old in churchyard-mould,
    He breedeth a mighty bow.
Alder for shoes do wise men choose,
    And beech for cups also.
But when ye have killed, and your bowl is spilled,
    And your shoes are clean outworn,
Back ye must speed for all that ye need
    To Oak, and Ash, and Thorn!

Ellum she hateth mankind, and waiteth
    Till every gust be laid
To drop a limb on the head of him
    That anyway trusts her shade.
But whether a lad be sober or sad,
    Or mellow with ale from the horn,
He will take no wrong when he lieth along
    'Neath Oak, and Ash, and Thorn!

Oh, do not tell the Priest our plight,
    Or he would call it a sin;
But—we have been out in the woods all night,
    A-conjuring Summer in!
And we bring you news by word of mouth—
    Good news for cattle and corn—
Now is the Sun come up from the South
    With Oak, and Ash, and Thorn!

Sing Oak, and Ash, and Thorn, good sirs
    (All of a Midsummer morn)!
England shall bide till Judgment Tide
    By Oak, and Ash, and Thorn!

Rudyard Kipling

A Tree Telling of Orpheus

White dawn. Stillness.   When the rippling began
    I took it for sea-wind, coming to our valley with rumors
    of salt, of treeless horizons. But the white fog
didn't stir; the leaves of my brothers remained outstretched,
unmoving.
        Yet the rippling drew nearer—and then
my own outermost branches began to tingle, almost as if
fire had been lit below them, too close, and their twig-tips
were drying and curling.
           Yet I was not afraid, only
           deeply alert.

I was the first to see him, for I grew
        out on the pasture slope, beyond the forest.
He was a man, it seemed: the two
moving stems, the short trunk, the two
arm-branches, flexible, each with five leafless
           twigs at their ends,
and the head that's crowned by brown or gold grass,
bearing a face not like the beaked face of a bird,
      more like a flower's.
          He carried a burden made of
some cut branch bent while it was green,
strands of a vine tight-stretched across it. From this,
when he touched it, and from his voice
which unlike the wind's voice had no need of our
leaves and branches to complete its sound,
            came the ripple.
But it was now no longer a ripple (he had come near and
stopped in my first shadow) it was a wave that bathed me
    as if rain
        rose from below and around me
    instead of falling.

And what I felt was no longer a dry tingling:
　　　　I seemed to be singing as he sang, I seemed to know
　　　　what the lark knows; all my sap
　　　　　　was mounting towards the sun that by now
　　　　　　　　had risen, the mist was rising, the grass
was drying, yet my roots felt music moisten them
deep under earth.

　　　　　He came still closer, leaned on my trunk:
　　　　　the bark thrilled like a leaf still-folded.
Music! There was no twig of me not
　　　　　　　　　　trembling with joy and fear.

Then as he sang
it was no longer sounds only that made the music:
he spoke, and as no tree listens I listened, and language
　　　　　　came into my roots
　　　　　　　　　　out of the earth,
　　　　　　　into my bark
　　　　　　　　　out of the air,
　　　　　　into the pores of my greenest shoots
　　　　　　　　gently as dew
and there was no word he sang but I knew its meaning.
He told of journeys,
　　　　　of where sun and moon go while we stand in dark,
　　of an earth-journey he dreamed he would take some day
deeper than roots . . .
He told of the dreams of man, wars, passions, griefs,
　　　　　and I, a tree, understood words—ah, it seemed
my thick bark would split like a sapling's that
　　　　　　　　　　grew too fast in the spring
when a late frost wounds it.

　　　　　　　　　Fire he sang,
that trees fear, and I, a tree, rejoiced in its flames.
New buds broke forth from me though it was full summer.

As though his lyre (now I knew its name)
were both frost and fire, its chords flamed
up to the crown of me.
I was seed again.
I was fern in the swamp.
I was coal.

And at the heart of my wood
(so close I was to becoming man or a god)
there was a kind of silence, a kind of sickness,
something akin to what men call boredom,
something
(the poem descended a scale, a stream over stones)
that gives to a candle a coldness
in the midst of its burning, he said.

It was then,
when in the blaze of his power that
reached me and changed me
I thought I should fall my length,
that the singer began
to leave me.   Slowly
moved from my noon shadow
to open light,
words leaping and dancing over his shoulders
back to me
rivery sweep of lyre-tones becoming
slowly again
ripple.

And I
in terror
but not in doubt of
what I must do
in anguish, in haste,
wrenched from the earth root after root,

the soil heaving and cracking, the moss tearing asunder—
and behind me the others: my brothers
forgotten since dawn. In the forest
they too had heard,
and were pulling their roots in pain
out of a thousand years' layers of dead leaves,
              rolling the rocks away,
                              breaking themselves
                                      out of
                                  their depths.
You would have thought we would lose the sound of the lyre,
                      of the singing
so dreadful the storm-sounds were, where there was no storm,
                  no wind but the rush of our
              branches moving, our trunks breasting the air.
              But the music!
                          The music reached us.

Clumsily,
          stumbling over our own roots,
              rustling our leaves

                                  in answer,
we moved, we followed.

All day we followed, up hill and down.
                          We learned to dance,
for he would stop, where the ground was flat,
                          and words he said
taught us to leap and to wind in and out
around one another   in figures   the lyre's measure designed.
The singer
          laughed till he wept to see us, he was so glad.
                                      At sunset
we came to this place I stand in, this knoll
with its ancient grove that was bare grass then.
          In the last light of that day his song became
farewell.
          He stilled our longing.
          He sang our sun-dried roots back into earth,

watered them: all-night rain of music so quiet
                                        we could almost
                not hear it in the
                                moonless dark.
By dawn he was gone.
                        We have stood here since,
in our new life.
                We have waited.
                                He does not return.
It is said he made his earth-journey, and lost
what he sought.
                It is said they felled him
and cut up his limbs for firewood.
                                And it is said
his head still sang and was swept out to sea singing.
Perhaps he will not return.
                        But what we have lived
comes back to us.
                We see more.
                                We feel, as our rings increase,
something that lifts our branches, that stretches our furthest
                                                leaf-tips
further.
        The wind, the birds,
                        do not sound poorer but clearer,
recalling our agony, and the way we danced.
The music!

Denise Levertov

The Tree-Trunks

How often were these trees
With multipartite vaults and traceries
Pillars of a cathedral
Aisled like Abingdon Church on Thames;
Now rusty gold crowns fall
From heads of old gods and their dames.

Here I am young again,
Young with the youth of Saturn's reign,
So young or old I feel that awe,
Spark in their night of nescience,
Men felt before they raised a saw
Or lying Homer passed his hat for pence.

Andrew Young

Two Japanese Maples

How can the snow,
Come all that way,
Remember to stay
In the twigs of these
Two delicate trees
In tufts just so
And be Japanese
And yet still know
With the dogwood and spruce
To flurry and play
As fast & loose
As the U.S.A.?

William Meredith

Under the Oak

You, if you were sensible,
When I tell you the stars flash signals, each one
    dreadful,
You would not turn and answer me
"The night is wonderful."

Even you, if you knew
How this darkness soaks me through and through,
    and infuses
Unholy fear in my essence, you would pause to
    distinguish
What hurts from what amuses.

For I tell you
Beneath this powerful tree, my whole soul's fluid
Oozes away from me as a sacrifice steam
At the knife of a Druid.

Again I tell you, I bleed, I am bound with withies,
My life runs out.
I tell you my blood runs out on the floor of this oak.
Gout upon gout.

Above me springs the blood-born mistletoe
In the shady smoke.
But who are you, twittering to and fro
Beneath the oak?

What thing better are you, what worse?
What have you to do with the mysteries
Of this ancient place, of my ancient curse?
What place have you in my histories?

D. H. Lawrence

Under Trees

Yellow tunnels under the trees, long avenues
Long as the whole of time:
A single aimless man
Carries a black garden broom.
He is too far to hear him
Wading through the leaves, down autumn
Tunnels, under yellow leaves, long avenues.

Geoffrey Grigson

Upper Lambourne

Up the ash-tree climbs the ivy,
    Up the ivy climbs the sun,
With a twenty-thousand pattering
    Has a valley breeze begun,
Feathery ash, neglected elder,
    Shift the shade and make it run—

Shift the shade toward the nettles,
    And the nettles set it free
To streak the stained Carrara headstone
    Where, in nineteen-twenty-three,
He who trained a hundred winners
    Paid the Final Entrance Fee.

Leathery limbs of Upper Lambourne,
    Leathery skin from sun and wind,
Leathery breeches, spreading stables,
    Shining saddles left behind—
To the down the string of horses
    Moving out of sight and mind.

Feathery ash in leathery Lambourne
    Waves above the sarsen stone,
And Edwardian plantations
    So coniferously moan
As to make the swelling downland,
    Far-surrounding, seem their own.

John Betjeman

Urgent

Villages pass under the plough
In England, where there was plague,
And lets time slide over parishes
The way hedges are torn out.
Bulldozers flatten a hill:
Even continents slip.
Everything must elide or kill
As the wild aurochs died;
And our elms. We have
Barely a minute now.

Sheila Wingfield

'The very leaves of the acacia-tree are London'

The very leaves of the acacia-tree are London;
London tap-water fills out the fuschia buds in the back garden,
Blackbirds pull London worms out of the sour soil,
The woodlice, centipedes, eat London, the wasps even.
London air through stomata of myriad leaves
And million lungs of London breathes.

Chlorophyll and haemoglobin do what life can
To purify, to return this great explosion
To sanity of leaf and wing.
Gradual and gentle the growth of London Pride,
And sparrows are free of all the time in the world:
Less than a window-pane between.

Kathleen Raine

Violet and Oak

Down through the trees is my green walk:
It is so narrow there and dark
That all the end, that's seen afar,
Is a dot of daylight, like a star.
When I had walked half-way or more,
I saw a pretty, small, blue flower;
And, looking closer, I espied
A small green stranger at her side.
If that flower's sweetheart lives to die
A natural death, thought I—
What will have happened by then
To a world of ever restless men?
'My little new-born oak,' I said,
'If my soul lives when I am dead,
I'll have an hour or more with you
Five hundred years from now!
When your straight back's so strong that though
Your leaves were lead on every bough,
It would not break—I'll think of you
When, weak and small, your sweetheart was
A little violet in the grass.'

W. H. Davies

Virgin in a Tree

How this tart fable instructs
And mocks! Here's the parody of that moral mousetrap
Set in the proverbs stitched on samplers
Approving chased girls who get them to a tree
And put on bark's nun-black

Habit which deflects
All amorous arrows. For to sheathe the virgin shape
In a scabbard of wood baffles pursuers,
Whether goat-thighed or god-haloed. Ever since that first Daphne
Switched her incomparable back

For a bay-tree hide, respect's
Twined to her hard limbs like ivy: the puritan lip
Cries: 'Celebrate Syrinx whose demurs
Won her the frog-colored skin, pale pith and watery
Bed of a reed. Look:

Pine-needle armor protects
Pitys from Pan's assault! And though age drop
Their leafy crown, their fame soars,
Eclipsing Eva, Cleo and Helen of Troy:
For which of those would speak

For a fashion that constricts
White bodies in a wooden girdle, root to top
Unfaced, unformed, the nipple-flowers
Shrouded to suckle darkness? Only they
Who keep cool and holy make

Over and over. And still the heaven
Of final surfeit is just as far
From the door as ever. What happens between us
Happens in darkness, vanishes
Easy and often as each breath.

Sylvia Plath

Walking in Autumn
for Diana Lodge

We have overshot the wood.
The track has led us beyond trees
to the tarmac edge. Too late now
at dusk to return a different way,
hazarding barbed wire or an unknown bull.
We turn back onto the darkening path.
Pale under-leaves of whitebeam, alder
gleam at our feet like stranded fish
or Hansel's stones.
A wren, unseen, churrs alarm:
each tree drains to blackness.
Halfway now, we know
by the leaning crab-apple:
feet crunching into mud
the hard slippery yellow moons.
We hurry without reason
stumbling over roots and stones.
A night creature lurches, cries out,
crashes through brambles.
Skin shrinks inside our clothes;
almost we run
falling through darkness to the wood's end,
the gate into the sloping field.
Home is lights and woodsmoke, voices—
and, our breath caught, not trembling now,
a strange reluctance to enter within doors.

Frances Horovitz

Walnut St., Oak St., Sycamore St., etc.

So this is what happened
to the names of the trees!
I heard them fly up,
whistling, out of the woods.
But I did not know
where they had gone.

Wendell Berry

'A waste of time! till Industry approached'

A waste of time! till Industry approached,
And roused him from his miserable sloth;
His faculties unfolded; pointed out
Where lavish Nature the directing hand
Of Art demanded; showed him how to raise
His feeble force by the mechanic powers,
To dig the mineral from the vaulted earth,
On what to turn the piercing rage of fire,
On what the torrent, and the gathered blast;
Gave the tall ancient forest to his axe;
Taught him to chip the wood, and hew the stone,
Till by degrees the finished fabric rose;
Tore from his limbs the blood-polluted fur,
And wrapt them in the woolly vestment warm,
Or bright in glossy silk, and flowing lawn;
With wholesome viands filled his table, poured
The generous glass around, inspired to wake
The life-refining soul of decent wit;
Nor stopped at barren bare necessity;
But, still advancing bolder, led him on
To pomp, to pleasure, elegance, and grace;
And, breathing high ambition through his soul,

Set science, wisdom, glory in his view,
And bade him be the lord of all below.
  Then gathering men their natural powers combined,
And formed a public; to the general good
Submitting, aiming, and conducting all.
For this the patriot-council met, the full,
The free, and fairly represented whole;
For this they planned the holy guardian laws,
Distinguished orders, animated arts,
And, with joint force Oppression chaining, set
Imperial Justice at the helm, yet still
To them accountable: nor slavish dreamed
That toiling millions must resign their weal
And all the honey of their search to such
As for themselves alone themselves have raised.
  Hence every form of cultivated life
In order set, protected, and inspired
Into perfection wrought. Uniting all,
Society grew numerous, high, polite,
And happy. Nurse of art, the city reared
In beauteous pride her tower-encircled head;
And, stretching street on street, by thousands drew,
From twining woody haunts, or the tough yew
To bows strong-straining, her aspiring sons.

James Thomson
from The Seasons: Autumn

The Way Through the Woods

They shut the road through the woods
Seventy years ago.
Weather and rain have undone it again,
And now you would never know
There was once a road through the woods
Before they planted the trees.

It is underneath the coppice and heath
And the thin anemones.
Only the keeper sees
That, where the ring-dove broods,
And the badgers roll at ease,
There was once a road through the woods.

Yet, if you enter the woods
Of a summer evening late,
When the night-air cools on the trout-ringed pools
Where the otter whistles his mate,
(They fear not men in the woods,
Because they see so few.)
You will hear the beat of a horse's feet,
And the swish of a skirt in the dew,
Steadily cantering through
The misty solitudes,
As though they perfectly knew
The old lost road through the woods . . .
But there is no road through the woods.

Rudyard Kipling

'When first the Eye this Forrest sees'

. . . When first the Eye this Forrest sees
It seems indeed as *Wood* not *Trees*:
As if their Neighbourhood so old
To one great Trunk them all did mold.
There the huge Bulk takes place, as ment
To thrust up a *Fifth Element*;
And stretches still so closely wedg'd
As if the Night within were hedg'd . . .

Andrew Marvell
from Upon Appleton House,
to my Lord Fairfax

175

'When there pressed in from the porch an appalling figure'

. . . When there pressed in from the porch an appalling figure,
Who in height outstripped all earthly men.
From throat to thigh he was thickset and square;
His loins and limbs were so long and great
That he was half a giant on earth, I believe,
Yet mainly and most of all a man he seemed,
And the handsomest of horsemen, though huge, at that;
For though at back and at breast his body was broad,
His hips and haunches were elegant and small,
And perfectly proportioned were all parts of the man,
    As seen.
   Amazed at the hue of him,
   A foe with furious mien,
   Men gaped, for the giant grim
   Was coloured a gorgeous green.

And garments of green girt the fellow about—
A two-third length tunic, tight at the waist,
A comely cloak on top, accomplished with lining
Of the finest fur to be found, manifest to all,
Marvellous fur-trimmed material, with matching hood
Lying back from his locks and laid on his shoulders;
Fitly held-up hose, in hue the same green,
That was caught at the calf, with clinking spurs beneath
Of bright gold on bases of embroidered silk,
With shields for the shanks and shins when riding.
And verily his vesture was all vivid green,
So were the bars on his belt and the brilliants set
In ravishing array on his rich accoutrements.
It would be tedious to tell a tithe of the trifles
Embossed and embroidered, such as birds and flies,
In green gay and gaudy, with gold in the middle,
About himself and his saddle on silken work.
The breast-hangings of the horse, its haughty crupper,
The enamelled knobs and nails on its bridle,

And the stirrups that he stood on, were all stained with the same;
So were the saddle-bows and splendid tail-straps,
That ever glimmered and glinted with their green stones.
The steed that he spurred on was similar in hue
    To the sight,
  Green and huge of grain,
  Mettlesome in might
  And brusque with bit and rein—
  A steed to serve that knight!

Yes, garbed all in green was the gallant rider.
His hair, like his horse in hue, hung light,
Clustering in curls like a cloak round his shoulders,
And a great bushy beard on his breast flowing down,
With the lovely locks hanging loose from his head,
Was shorn below the shoulder, sheared right round,
So that half his arms were under the encircling hair,
Covered as by a king's cape, that closes at the neck.
The mane of that mighty horse, much like the beard,
Well crisped and combed, was copiously plaited
With twists of twining gold, twinkling in the green,
First a green gossamer, a golden one next.
His flowing tail and forelock followed suit,
And both were bound with bands of bright green,
Ornamented to the end with exquisite stones,
While a thong running thwart threaded on high
Many bright golden bells, burnished and ringing.
Such a horse, such a horseman, in the whole wide world
Was never seen or observed by those assembled before,
    Not one.
  Lightning-like he seemed
  And swift to strike and stun.
  His dreadful blows, men deemed,
  Once dealt, meant death was done.

Yet hauberk and helmet had he none,
Nor plastron nor plate-armour proper to combat,
Nor shield for shoving, nor sharp spear for lunging;
But he held a holly cluster in one hand, holly

That is greenest when groves are gaunt and bare,
And an axe in his other hand, huge and monstrous,
An axe fell and fearsome, fit for a fable;
For fully forty inches frowned the head.
Its handle-base was hued in green, in hammered gold and steel.
The blade was burnished bright, with a broad edge,
Acutely honed for cutting, as keenest razors are.
The grim man gripped it by its great strong handle,
Which was wound with iron all the way to the end,
And graven in green with graceful designs . . .

Anon
from Sir Gawain and the Green Knight

Wind and Tree

In the way that the most of the wind
Happens where there are trees,

Most of the world is centred
About ourselves.

Often where the wind has gathered
The trees together and together,

One tree will take
Another in her arms and hold.

Their branches that are grinding
Madly together and together,

It is no real fire.
They are breaking each other.

Often I think I should be like
The single tree, going nowhere,

Since my own arm could not and would not
Break the other. Yet by my broken bones

I tell new weather.

Paul Muldoon

A Wind Flashes the Grass

Leaves pour blackly across.
We cling to the earth, with glistening eyes, pierced afresh by the
tree's cry.

And the incomprehensible cry
From the boughs, in the wind
Sets us listening for below words,
Meanings that will not part from the rock.

The trees thunder in unison, on a gloomy afternoon
And the ploughman grows anxious, his tractor becomes terrible.
His memory litters downwind
And the shadow of his bones tosses darkly on the air.

The trees suddenly storm to a stop, in a hush
Against the sky, where the field ends.
They crowd there shuddering
And wary, like horses bewildered by lightning.

The stirring of their twigs against the dark, travelling sky
Is the oracle of the earth.

They too are afraid they too are momentary
Streams rivers of shadow

Ted Hughes

Winter

The tree still bends over the lake,
And I try to recall our love,
Our love which had a thousand leaves.

Sheila Wingfield

Winter the Huntsman

Through his iron glades
Rides Winter the Huntsman.
All colour fades
As his horn is heard sighing.

Far through the forest
His wild hooves crash and thunder
Till many a mighty branch
Is torn asunder.

And the red reynard creeps
To his hole near the river,
The copper leaves fall
And the bare trees shiver.

As night creeps from the ground,
Hides each tree from its brother,
And each dying sound
Reveals yet another.

Is it Winter the Huntsman
Who gallops through his iron glades,
Cracking his cruel whip
To the gathering shades?

Osbert Sitwell

The Winter Trees

Against the evening sky the trees are black,
Iron themselves against the iron rails;
The hurrying crowds seek cinemas or homes,
A cosy hour where warmth will mock the wind.
They do not look at trees now summer's gone,
For fallen with their leaves are those glad days
Of sand and sea and ships, of swallows, lambs,
Of cricket teams, and walking long in woods.

Standing among the trees, a shadow bends
And picks a cigarette-end from the ground;
It lifts the collar of an overcoat,
And blows upon its hands and stamps its feet—
For this is winter, chastiser of the free,
This is the winter, kind only to the bound.

Clifford Dyment

Winter Trees

The wet dawn inks are doing their blue dissolve.
On their blotter of fog the trees
Seem a botanical drawing—
Memories growing, ring on ring,
A series of weddings.

Knowing neither abortions nor bitchery,
Truer than women,
They seed so effortlessly!
Tasting the winds, that are footless,
Waist-deep in history—

Full of wings, otherwordliness.
In this, they are Ledas.
O mother of leaves and sweetness
Who are these pietàs?
The shadows of ringdoves chanting, but easing nothing.

Sylvia Plath

The Wood

A wood.
A man entered;
thought he knew the way
through. The old furies
attended. Did he emerge
in his right mind? The same
man? How many years
passed? Aeons? What is
the right mind? What does
'same' mean? No change of clothes
for the furies? Fast
as they are cut down
the trees grow, new
handles for axes.
There is a rumour from the heart
of the wood: brow
furrowed, mind
smooth, somebody huddles
in wide contemplation—Buddha,
Plato, Blake, Jung—
the name changes, identity
remains, pure being waiting
to be come at. Is it the self
that he mislaid? Is it why

he entered, ignoring
the warning of the labyrinth
without end? How many times
over must he begin again?

R. S. *Thomas*

'The wooden-shouldered tree is wild and high'

The wooden-shouldered tree is wild and high,
it is a plane-tree lighted inwardly,
it imprisons the sun in a cloth of leaf.
That will escape from this world though,
the tree is deliberate, it is life,
it has a musty smell and a shadow.

Bigger breasted than birds, it is breathing,
hangs with a weightless weight on everything,
having considered the sun from time to time
which vanishes in incense and yellow light:
is as silent as fog, the winter gleam
of a small sun and the birds in their flight.

It is courageous and it is alive,
this tree is nine parts of what I believe:
freedom lies in the inward of nature,
and this tree is green fire in a world of trees,
catches blue air, is neither pure nor impure,
but is alive. It is alive and dies.

Peter Levi

Wooding

From windows in the Home, old people
stared across the park, watching us
force rhododendron branches back
and trample nettles till the cedar logs

appeared. We must have looked minute:
a father and two sons no more than silhouettes
which stooped, and staggered comically
to where a trailer stood half darkened

by the wall. It took an hour.
And afterwards, to see us fooling
round the green wet-smelling load,
they would have thought us happy.

There we were: me running, my brother
kicking leaves, and each of us decked out
with split sweet chestnut husks
as spiky nipples on our coats.

The whole short afternoon we spoke
of anything except your death,
and then, next day, beyond that
blank enormous wall we buried you,

still destitute of ways to show our grief.

Andrew Motion

The Wood of the Self-Murdered

The trees against the mountain's groin
Pitch wigwams in a zigzag line.
Pelts of pine and spruce and fir
Are tented in the cloudy air;
The western light slides down the wide
Slant of the branches of brown hide.

No creature tracks the furry dark,
Not owl nor weasel is awake;
The wind grunts by and rubs its flanks
And hears the groans of rocking trunks,
And the dead drip of the red rain
As the mist blankets down again.

On every twig and branch are risen
Blobs of blood like dark red resin
That drizzle to the ground and stain
Grass and brambleleaf and thorn;
The bark is blistered and the wood
Crusted with scabs and boils of blood.

These are the wooden souls of men
Who broke the life in their own bone;
With rope round neck or knife in throat
They turned their backs upon the light,
And now their fears creak in the breeze,
In blood-red darkness, turned to trees.

Beneath the soil the long shoots bore
To limestone and to iron ore,
Where through the rock that waters ooze
Red as the sap in the live trees,
And becks swill seaward, rich as wine,
The haemorrhage of the split mine.

Empires and towns are buried here
That stabbed themselves or died of fear.
Towers and terraces crack and fall,
And sink into the sandy soil,
And, bleeding like a running sore,
Do penance in the broken ore.

Norman Nicholson

Wood Rides

Who hath not felt the influence that so calms
The weary mind in summers sultry hours
When wandering thickest woods beneath the arms
Of ancient oaks and brushing nameless flowers
That verge the little ride who hath not made
A minutes waste of time and sat him down
Upon a pleasant swell to gaze awhile
On crowding ferns bluebells and hazel leaves
And showers of lady smocks so called by toil
When boys sprote gathering sit on stulps and weave
Garlands while barkmen pill the fallen tree
—Then mid the green variety to start
Who hath (not) met that mood from turmoil free
And felt a placid joy refreshed at heart

John Clare

Woods

I part the out thrusting branches
and come in beneath
the blessed and the blessing trees.
Though I am silent
there is singing around me.
Though I am dark
there is vision around me.
Though I am heavy
there is flight around me.

Wendell Berry

'Ye fallen avenues! once more I mourn'

Ye fallen avenues! once more I mourn
Your fate unmerited, once more rejoice
That yet a remnant of your race survives.
How airy and how light the graceful arch,
Yet awful as the consecrated roof
Re-echoing pious anthems! while beneath
The chequer'd earth seems restless as a flood
Brush'd by the wind. So sportive is the light
Shot through the boughs, it dances as they dance,
Shadow and sunshine intermingling quick,
And darkening and enlightening, as the leaves
Play wanton, every moment, every spot.

William Cowper
from The Task

'You lingering sparse leaves of me on winter-nearing boughs'

You lingering sparse leaves of me on winter-nearing boughs,
And I some well-shorn tree of field or orchard-row;
You tokens diminute and lorn—(not now the flush of May,
    or July clover-bloom—no grain of August now;)
You pallid banner-staves—you pennants valueless—you
    over-stay'd of time,
Yet my soul-dearest leaves confirming all the rest,
The faithfulest—hardiest—last.

Walt Whitman

'Y was a Yew'

Y was a yew,
Which flourished and grew,
By a quiet abode
Near the side of a road.

y!
Dark little Yew!

Edward Lear

Acknowledgements

It seemed a simple journey—but once we had begun we were overwhelmed with the diversity of routes we could take.

We have to heap thanks upon Susan Forrester and Kim Taplin for sending us along some of the richest paths. Kim has written an inspirational book *Tongues in Trees: Trees in the English literary imagination* (Green Books 1989). We are grateful to the Arts Council for the wonderful 20th century Poetry Library now at the South Bank Centre and to the Library of University College London. Michael Bird, Kim Richardson and everyone at Bristol Classical Press deserve our thank for their helpfulness and cheerful patience, and Simon Bishop who designed the cover of this book and *In A Nutshell*. We are grateful to Angela Verren-Taunt for so generously allowing us to use the wonderful Ben Nicholson tree extensively in our Trees, Woods and the Green Man campaign which has been funded by the London Boroughs Grant Scheme, the Department of the Environment, the Nature Conservancy Council, The Ernest Cook Trust and a London-based Trust.

John Fowles' writing, with its powerful allusions to nature, has been important to us for a long time—we are very grateful for a provocative Foreword.

Our greatest thanks, of course, must go to the poets, from our contemporaries to those whose names we will never know, for giving us such riches. We thank all the poets, publishers and executors who have kindly given permission, and particularly Mavis Pindard at Faber and Faber for friendly, clear and candid help when we first entered the copyright jungle. We have had many warm letters and good wishes: thank you all.

Out of 900 poems with trees at their centre that we found on this first foray we have had to leave out many favourites—but we hope that the breadth and variety of this, our selection, gives pause for thought and lures you to further reading; with this in mind we include formal copyright acknowledgements with full references below. These pages form an extension of the copyright page. We have tried very hard to trace copyright holders—we apologise if there are any omissions or mistakes. We would be grateful if you could write to us so that we can correctly attribute and thank the people concerned.

Angela King and Susan Clifford
1989

Acknowledgements
to the Second Edition

We reiterate the thanks we offered in the first edition, especially to the poets who have been so warm and generous and we are similarly grateful to John Fowles for letting us include his Foreword again, with a few small amendments.

Clifford Harper has been good enough to complete his set of images in this trilogy of anthologies by creating an illustration for the cover in homage to the Ben Nicholson tree which launched the first edition.

Thank you to William Heyen and his publishers for the poem 'Emancipation Proclamation', published after our first edition in *Pterodactyl Rose — Poems of Ecology*, Time Being Books 1991. Although we have included no other newer poems, we felt its powerful eloquence so important that we have given it pride of place in our preface.

John Elford and the team at Green Books have been great stalwarts and we are particularly grateful to them for giving us the chance to see *Trees be Company* in print once more to make up the set of three anthologies with *Field Days* and *The River's Voice*.

We have once more searched high and low to renew permissions. Please get in touch if we have failed to reach copyright holders; much has changed since the first edition.

Angela King and Susan Clifford
2001

A–Z List of Poets and their Poems with Sources and Acknowledgements

Anon
'In somer, when the shawes be sheyne'
from The Ballad of Robyn Hode and the Munke (traditional)
The Oxford Book of Ballads ed. J. Kinsley, Oxford University
Press 1969.

'Hwaet! A dream came to me at deep midnight'
from The Dream of the Rood (pre-7th century)
The Earliest English Poets translated & introduced by Michael
Alexander, Penguin Classics 1966, 1977. © Michael Alexander
1966, 1977, 1991; reproduced by permission of Penguin UK.

'The holly and the ivy (traditional)
The Oxford Book of Carols by P. Dearmer, R. Vaughan Williams
and M. Shaw, Oxford University Press 1928.

Glyn Cynon Wood (16th century)

Never Tell (13th century)
Oxford Book of Welsh Verse in English Oxford University Press
1983.

'When there pressed in from the porch an appalling figure' *from*
Sir Gawain and the Green Knight translated by Brian Stone,
Penguin Classics 1959, 1974. © Brian Stone 1959, 1964, 1974.
Reproduced by Permission of Penguin UK.

Abse, Dannie, 1923–
Tree
White Coat, Purple Coat Hutchinson 1989 and Persea Books U.S.
1989. © Dannie Abse & Hutchinson 1989. Reprinted by
permission of the author.

Ashbery, John, 1927–
Some Trees
Selected Poems Carcanet Press 1986. © 1956 by John Ashbery.
Reprinted by permission of Georges Borchardt Inc for the author
and Carcanet Press Ltd.

Barnes, William, 1801–1886
Trees Be Company
William Barnes—The Dorset Poet The Dovecote Press 1984.
Reproduced by permission of the Dovecote Press.

Belloc, Hilaire, 1870–1953
The Elm
Complete Verse Random House UK Ltd © H. Belloc 1970,
reproduced by permission of the Estate of Hilaire Belloc and PFD.

Berry, Wendell, 1934–
Walnut St., Oak St., Sycamore St., etc.
Ronsard's Lament for the Cutting of the Forest of Gastine Woods
A Part North Point Press 1980. © Wendell Berry 1980. Reprinted
by permission of the author.

'How long does it take to make the woods'
Sabbaths North Point Press 1987. © Wendell Berry 1987.
Reprinted by permission of the author.

Planting Trees
The Old Elm Tree by the River
Collected Poems 1957–82 North Point Press 1985. © Wendell
Berry 1985. Reprinted by permission of the author.

Betjeman, John, 1906–1984
Upper Lambourne
John Betjeman's Collected Poems John Murray 1980. © John
Betjeman 1980. Reprinted by permission John Murray
(Publishers) Ltd.

Blake, William 1757–1827
A Poison Tree
Songs of Experience
The Complete Writings of William Blake ed. G. Keynes, Oxford
University Press 1966.

Blunden, Edmund, 1896–1974
The Tree in the Goods Yard
After the Bombing Macmillan 1949. © Edmund Blunden 1949.

Timber
Selected Poems Carcanet Press 1982. © Edmund Blunden 1944.
Reprinted by permission of the PFD on behalf of the Estate of Mrs
Claire Blunden and Carcanet Press Ltd.

Brooke, Rupert, 1887–1915
Pine-Trees and the Sky: Evening
The Poetical Works of Rupert Brooke ed. Geoffrey Keynes, Faber
& Faber 1946.

Browning, Robert, 1812–1889
Home-Thoughts, From Abroad
Poetical Works 1833–1864 ed. Ian Jack, Oxford Univ. Press 1970.

Casey, Mary, 1915–1980
Not After Plutarch
Full Circle The Enitharmon Press 1981. © Mary Casey 1981.
Reproduced by permission of the Enitharmon Press.

Causley, Charles, 1917–
Green Man in the Garden
Collected Poems Macmillan 1975. © Charles Causley 1975.
Reproduced by permission of David Higham Associates.

Chaucer, Geoffrey, 1340?–1400
'The solemn work of building up the pyre'
from The Knight's Tale, *The Canterbury Tales* translated by Nevill
Coghill, Penguin Classics 1951, 1977. © Nevill Coghill 1951,
1958, 1960, 1975, 1977. Reproduced by permission of Penguin
UK.

'For over-al, wher that I myn eyen caste'
from The Parlement of Foules. *Chaucer—Complete Works* ed.
Walter Skent, Oxford University Press 1976.

Clare, John, 1793–1864
The Fallen Elm
Wood Rides
John Clare The Midsummer Cushion ed. A. Tibble, Mid
Northumberland Arts Group & Carcanet Press 1979. Reprinted
by permission of Carcanet Press Ltd.

Clarke, Gillian, 1937–
Cardiff Elms
Selected Poems Carcanet Press 1985. © Gillian Clarke 1985.
Thanks to the author & Carcanet Press.

Cowper, William, 1731–1800
The Poplar Field
'Survivor sole, and hardly such, of all' *from* Yardley Oak
'Ye fallen avenues! once more I mourn'
'Nor less attractive is the woodland scene'
from The Task I & II
Oxford University Press, various sources

Davies, W. H., 1870–1940
No-man's Wood
Violet and Oak
The Old Oak Tree
The Complete Poems of W. H. Davies Jonathan Cape 1963.
© W. H. Davies and Jonathan Cape Ltd 1963; with thanks to the
Mrs H. M. Davies Will Trust, Jonathan Cape, and Wesleyan
University Press.

Day Lewis, C., 1904–1972
The Christmas Tree
Maple and Sumach
The Complete Poems of C. Day Lewis Sinclair-Stevenson 1992.
© 1992 in this edition, and the Estate of C. Day Lewis.
Reproduced by permission of the Random House Group.

Drummond, William, 1585–1649
'Thrise happie hee, who by some shadie Grove'

Duffy, Maureen, 1933–
Song of the Stand Pipe
Tree Fall
Collected Poems 1949–84 Hamish Hamilton 1985. © Maureen
Duffy 1985. Reproduced by permission of the author.

Dunn, Douglas, 1942–
Dieback
Northlight Faber & Faber 1988. © Douglas Dunn 1988.
Reprinted by permission of PFD and Faber & Faber Ltd.

Dyment, Clifford, 1914–1970
The Winter Trees
Collected Poems by Clifford Dyment J.M. Dent 1970. © Clifford
Dyment 1970. Reproduced by permission of The Orion Publishing
Group Ltd.

Fainlight, Ruth, 1931–
The New Tree
Sibyls and Others Hutchinson 1980. © Ruth Fainlight 1980.
Reproduced by permission of the author.

Trees
Selected Poems Sinclair-Stevenson 1995. © Ruth Fainlight 1995.
Reproduced by permission of the author.

Feinstein, Elaine, 1930–
The Magic Apple Tree
Selected Poems Carcanet Press 1994. © Elaine Feinstein 1971.
Reprinted by permission of Carcanet Press Ltd.

Frost, Robert, 1874–1963
Birches
On a Tree Fallen Across the Road
The Poetry of Robert Frost ed. Edward Connery Lathem,
Jonathan Cape 1971. © Robert Frost 1971. With thanks to the
Estate of Robert Frost and to Jonathan Cape Ltd.

Fuller, John, 1937–
The Elms
Living a good way up a mountain'
Collected Poems Chatto & Windus 1996. © John Fuller 1972,
1988. Reproduced by permission of the author.

Ginsberg, Allen, 1926–1997
'Autumn again, you wouldn't know in the city'
from Autumn Gold: New England Fall
Collected Poems 1947–80, Penguin Books 1997. © Allen Ginsberg
1971, 1996. Reproduced by permission of HarperCollins
Publishers Inc. and Penguin UK.

Gogarty, O. St. John, 1878–1957
The Crab Tree
Selected Poems Macmillan 1933. © Gogarty 1933.

Graves, Robert, 1895–1985
An English Wood
The Complete Poems of Robert Graves edited by Beryl Graves
and Dunstan Ward, Carcanet Press Ltd 1995. © Robert Graves
1958.

The Battle of the Trees
The White Goddess Faber & Faber 1961. © Robert Graves 1961.
Reproduced by permission of Carcanet Press Ltd.

Grigson, Geoffrey, 1905–1985
Elms under Cloud
Under Trees
The Collected Works of Geoffrey Grigson 1924–62 Phoenix
House 1963. © Geoffrey Grigson 1963. Reproduced by
permission of David Higham Associates.

Gunn, Thom, 1929–
The Cherry Tree
Complete Poems by Thom Gunn Faber & Faber 1993. © Thom
Gunn 1994. Reprinted by permission of Faber & Faber Ltd and
Farrar, Straus and Giroux, LLC.

Gurney, Ivor, 1890–1937
Felling a Tree
Collected Poems of Ivor Gurney Oxford University Press 1984.

Hamburger, Michael, 1924–
Oak
Collected Poems 1941–1994 Anvil Press Poetry 1995. © Michael
Hamburger 1988. Reproduced by permission of the author and
Anvil Press Poetry Ltd.

Hardy, Thomas, 1840–1928
In a Wood
Throwing a Tree
To a Tree in London (Clement's Inn)
The Variorum Edition of the Complete Poems of Thomas Hardy
ed. James Gibson, Macmillan 1979.

Harrison, Heather, 1943–
Green Man
Roots Beneath The Pavement (West Midlands Arts and Common
Ground) Birmingham Readers & Writers Festival 1987. © Heather
Harrison 1987. Reproduced by permission of the author.

Harrison, Tony, 1937–
Cypress & Cedar
Selected Poems Penguin 1987. © Tony Harrison 1987.
Reproduced by permission of the author.

Heaney, Seamus, 1939–
Bog Oak
The Plantation
Opened Ground: Selected Poems 1966–1996 Faber & Faber
1998. © Seamus Heaney 1998. Reprinted by permission of the
author, Faber & Faber Ltd and Farrar Straus and Giroux, LLC.

'The bushy leafy oak tree'
from *Sweeney Astray: A Version From The Irish* translated by
Seamus Heaney, A Field Day Publication 1983. © Seamus Heaney
1983.

Heath-Stubbs, John, 1918–
'This night I walk through a forest in my head'
from The Heart's Forest
Collected Poems 1943–87 Carcanet Press 1988. © John
Heath-Stubbs 1988. Reproduced by permission of David Higham
Associates.

Herbert, George, 1593–1633
'Now I am here what thou wilt do with me'
from The Temple (Affliction 1)
The Works of George Herbert Oxford University Press 1941.

Herrick, Robert, 1591–1674
Ceremonies for Candlemasse Eve
The Poetical Works of Robert Herrick Oxford University Press
1915.

Heyen, William, 1940–
The Elm's Home
Maple and Starlings
Long Island Light: Poems and A Memoir The Vanguard Press Inc.
New York 1979. © William Heyen 1979. Reproduced by
permission of the author.

Horovitz, Frances, 1938–83
Walking in Autumn
Collected Poems Bloodaxe Books 1985. © Frances Horovitz 1985.
With thanks to Roger Garfitt and Bloodaxe Books.

Housman, A. E., 1859–1936
'Give me a land of boughs in leaf'
'Loveliest of trees, the cherry now'
from A Shropshire Lad
The Collected Works of A. E. Housman Jonathan Cape 1939.
Reproduced by permission of The Society of Authors as the
literary representative of the estate of A. E. Housman.

Hughes, Ted, 1930–1999
'I see the oak's bride in the oak's grasp' *from* Gaudete
'A Wind Flashes the Grass' *from* Wodwo
Selected Poems 1957–81 Faber & Faber 1982. © Ted Hughes
1982.

A Tree
Remains of Elmet Faber & Faber 1979. © Ted Hughes 1979.
Reprinted by permission of Faber & Faber Ltd.

Hyland, Paul 1947–
To Make a Tree
The Stubborn Forest Bloodaxe Books 1984. © Paul Hyland 1994.
Reproduced by permission of the author.

Jennings, Elizabeth, 1926–
Beech
Growing Points, Collected Poems Carcanet Press 1975.
© Elizabeth Jennings 1975. Reproduced by permission of David
Higham Associates.

Jonson, Ben, 1573–1637
'It is not growing like a tree'
The Complete Works of Ben Jonson ed. William Hunter, New
York University Press 1963.

Kavanagh, Patrick, 1904–67
Beech Tree
To A Late Poplar
The Complete Poems of Patrick Kavanagh edited by Peter
Kavanagh, Hand Press 1977, 250 East 30th Street, New York
10016. © Peter Kavanagh 1972.

Poplar Memory
Selected Poems of Patrick Kavanagh edited by Dr Antoinette
Quinn, Penguin 1996. © Patrick Kavanagh 1972. Reprinted with
the permission of the Trustees of the Estate of the late Katherine B.
Kavanagh, through the Jonathan Williams Literary Agency.

Kavanagh, P. J., 1931–
A Single Tree
Elder
Collected Poems Carcanet 1992 © P. J. Kavanagh 1987.
Reproduced by permission of the author.

Kilmer, A. Joyce, 1886–1918
'I think that I shall never see'

Kipling, R., 1865–1936
A Tree Song
The Way Through the Woods
Rudyard Kipling's Verse Definitive Edition Hodder and Stoughton
1912. Reproduced by permission of A. P. Watt Ltd on behalf of
the National Trust.

Kitchener Davies, J., 1902–52
'The Land of Y Llian was on the high marsh'
from The Sound of the Wind that is Blowing
The Oxford Book of Welsh Verse in English Oxford University
Press 1983. With thanks to Mrs Mair I. Davies for permission to
extract Sion y Gwynt sy'n Chwytha © J. Kitchener Davies 1983;
translated by J. P. Clancy.

Larkin, Philip, 1922–1985
The Trees
Collected Poems Faber & Faber 1974. © 1988, 1989 by the Estate
of Philip Larkin. Reprinted by permission of Faber & Faber Ltd
and Farrar, Straus and Giroux, LLC.

Lawrence, D. H., 1885–1930
Bare Almond-Trees
Delight Of Being Alone
Under The Oak

The Complete Poems of D. H. Lawrence edited by V. de Sola Pinto and F. W. Roberts. © 1964, 1971 by Angelo Ravaglio & C. M. Weekley, Executors of the Estate of Freda Lawrence Ravagli. Used by permission of Viking Penguin, a division of Penguin Putnam Inc.

Lear, Edward, 1812–1888
'There was an old lady whose folly'
Bosh & Nonsense Allen Lane 1982.

'There was an old man in a Tree'
'Y was a yew'
The Complete Nonsense of Edward Lear ed. Holbrook Jackson, Faber & Faber Ltd 1947.

Levertov, Denise, 1923–1998
A Tree Telling of Orpheus
Poems 1968–72, A New Directions Book. © Denise Levertov Goodman 1970. Reprinted by permission of Laurence Pollinger Ltd and New Directions Publishing Corp.

Levi, Peter, 1931–2000
Alcaic
'In midwinter a wood was'
'The wooden-shouldered tree is wild and high'
Collected Poems 1955–75 Anvil Press Poetry 1984. © Peter Levi 1976. Reproduced by permission of Anvil Press Poetry Ltd.

Llewellyn-Williams, Hilary, 1951–
Oak Duir
Tree Calendar Poetry Wales Press 1987. © Hilary Llewellyn-William 1987.

Lowell, Robert, 1917–1977
'No weekends for the gods now. Wars'
excerpt from Waking Early Sunday Morning
Near the Ocean Faber and Faber 1967. © Robert Lowell 1967. Reprinted by permission of Faber & Faber and Farrar, Straus and Giroux, LLC.

MacNeice, Louis, 1907–1963
The Tree of Guilt
Tree Party
The Collected Poems of Louis MacNeice Faber & Faber 1966. © Louis MacNeice 1966. Reprinted by permission of David Higham Associates.

Manley Hopkins, Gerard, 1844–1889
Binsey Poplars
Poems and Prose selected and edited by W.H. Gardner, Penguin 1953/63.

Marvell, Andrew, 1621–1678
'When first the Eye this Forrest sees'
from Upon Appleton House, to my Lord Fairfax
The Poems & Letters of Andrew Marvell, Vol I—Poems Oxford University Press 1927.

Meredith, George, 1828–1909
'Enter these enchanted woods'
from The Woods of Westermain, Poems and Lyrics of the Joy of the Earth
Poems Volume II The Times Book Club 1912.

Meredith, William, 1919–
Two Japanese Maples
The Wreck of the Thresher and Other Poems Alfred A. Knopf, New York 1964. © William Meredith 1964. All rights reserved; reprinted by permission of the author.

Mew, Charlotte, 1869–1928
Afternoon Tea
Domus Caedet Arborem
Collected Poems & Prose Carcanet Press 1981. Reprinted by permission of Carcanet Press Ltd.

Milligan, Spike, 1918–
Tree-kill
Unspun Socks From a Children's Laundry & Other Children's Verse M. & J. Hobbs in association with Michael Joseph 1991. © Spike Milligan 1981. Reprinted by permission of the author.

Morrison, Blake, 1950–
Pine
Dark Glasses Chatto & Windus 1984. © Blake Morrison 1984. Reproduced by permission of PFD.

Motion, Andrew, 1952–
Wooding
Dangerous Play: Poems 1974–1984 Penguin 1984. © Andrew Motion 1984. Reprinted by permission of PFD.

Muldoon, Paul, 1951–
Wind and Tree
Selected Poems 1968–83 Faber & Faber 1986. © Paul Muldoon
1973. Reprinted by permission Faber & Faber Ltd and the author.

Nash, Ogden, 1902–1971
Song of the Open Road
Collected Verse from 1929 on J. M. Dent 1966. © Ogden Nash
1966. Reproduced by permission of Curtis Brown, New York.

Nicholson, Norman, 1914–1997
The Elm Decline
A Local Habitation Faber & Faber 1972. © Norman Nicholson
1972.

The Wood of the Self-Murdered
Five Rivers Faber & Faber 1944. © Norman Nicholson 1944;
reprinted by permission of David Higham Associates.

Pitter, Ruth, 1897–1992
The Cedar
The Tall Fruit-Trees
Collected Poems Enitharmon Press 1996. © Ruth Pitter 1968;
reprinted by permission of Enitharmon Press.

Plath, Sylvia, 1932–1963
Virgin in a Tree
Winter Trees
The Collected Poems of Sylvia Plath ed. Ted Hughes, Faber &
Faber 1981. © 1960, 1965, 1971, 1981 by the Estate of Sylvia
Plath. Editorial material © Ted Hughes. Reproduced by permission
of Faber & Faber Ltd and HarperCollins Publishers.

Porteous, Katrina, 1960–
Tree of Heaven
The Lost Music Bloodaxe Books 1996. © Katrina Porteous 1989.
Reproduced by permission of the author.

Pound, Ezra, 1885–1972
The Tree
Collected Shorter Poems by Ezra Pound Faber & Faber 1949.
© Ezra Pound 1949. Reprinted by permission of Faber & Faber
Ltd and New Directions Publishing Corporation.

Raine, Craig, 1944–
In The Woods
The Onion, Memory Oxford University Press 1978.
© Craig Raine 1978. Reprinted by permission of the author.

Raine, Kathleen, 1908–
   London Trees
   The Trees in Tubs
   Collected Poems Hamish Hamilton 1956. © Kathleen Raine 1956.

   The Leaf
   'The very leaves of the acacia-tree are London'
   Poems from The Oval Portrait Hamish Hamilton 1977.
   © Kathleen Raine 1977. Reproduced by permission of the author.

Salzman, Eva, 1960–
   Ending Up in Kent
   The English Earthquake Bloodaxe Books 1992. © Eva Salzman
   1987. Reproduced by permission of the author.

Sassoon, Siegfried, 1886–1967
   Blunden's Beech
   South Wind
   Collected Poems of Siegfried Sassoon © 1918, 1920 by E.P.
   Dutton, © 1936, 1946, 1947, 1948 by Siegfried Sassoon.
   Used by permission of Viking Penguin, a division of Penguin
   Putnam Inc, and by kind permission of George Sassoon.

Scannell, Vernon, 1922–
   Apple Poem
   Collected Poems 1950–1993 Robson Books 1993. © Vernon
   Scannell 1987. With thanks to the author & Robson Books Ltd.

Shakespeare, William, 1564–1616
   'Now, my co mates and brothers-in-exile'
   'O Rosalind,
   As You Like It

   'There is an old tale goes that Herne the Hunter'
   The Merry Wives of Windsor

Sitwell, Osbert, 1892–1969
   extract from Winter The Huntsman
   Selected Poems Old & New Duckworth 1943. © Osbert Sitwell
   1943. Reproduced by permission of David Higham Associates.

Smith, Stevie, 1902–1971
   Alone in the Woods
   The Collected Poems of Stevie Smith Penguin Modern Classics
   1985. © Stevie Smith 1985. With thanks to James MacGibbon,
   © Stevie Smith 1972. Reproduced by permission of New
   Directions Publishing Corp. and the Estate of James MacGibbon.

Snyder, Gary, 1930–
'The groves are down' *from* Logging
Myths & Texts Totem Books in association with Corinth Books
1960. © Gary Snyder 1960. Reproduced by permission of the
author.

Fence Posts
Axe Handles North Point Press 1983. © Gary Snyder 1983.
Reprinted by permission of North Point Press, a division of Farrar,
Straus and Giroux, LLC and the author.

Stovewood
Regarding Wave New Directions 1967. © Gary Snyder 1967.
Reproduced by permission of the author.

Spenser, Edmund, 1552–1599
'There grew a goodly tree him faire beside'
from The Faerie Queene
Spenser's Poetical Works Oxford University Press 1912.

Stallworthy, Jon, 1935–
A Barbican Ash
Root & Branch Chatto & Windus 1969. © Jon Stallworthy 1969.
Reproduced by permission of The Random House Group.

Szirtes, George, 1948–
The Silver Tree
November & May Secker & Warburg 1981. © George Szirtes
1981. Reproduced by permission of the author.

Taplin, Kim, 1943–
The May-Tree
First published in *Peace News*. © Kim Taplin 1987. reproduced by
permission of the author.

Tennyson, Alfred Lord, 1809–1892
Amphion
'Old Yew, which graspeth at the stones'
from In Memoriam A. H. H.
The Poems of Tennyson Longman 1969.

Thomas , Dylan, 1914–1953
'Shut, too, in a tower of words, I mark'
from Especially when the October wind
Collected Poems 1934–52 J. M. Dent 1952. © Dylan Thomas
1952. *The Poems of Dylan Thomas* © 1939 by New Directions
Publishing Corporation. Reprinted by permission of New
Directions and Laurence Pollinger Ltd.

Thomas Edward, 1878–1917
The Chalk-Pit
The Cherry Trees
The Combe
Fifty Faggots
The Collected Poems of Edward Thomas Oxford University Press
1978. Reproduced by permission of Mfanwy Thomas.

Thomas, R. S., 1913–2000
Afforestation
The Bread of Truth Rupert Hart-Davis 1964. © R. S. Thomas
1964. Reproduced by permission from Grafton Books, a division
of the Collins Publishing Group.

The Wood
Experimenting with an Amen Macmillan 1986. © R. S. Thomas
1986.

Thomson, James, 1700–1748
'Bear me, Pomona! to thy citron groves'
'A waste of time! Till Industry approached'
The Seasons (extracts from Summer & Autumn).

Thwaite, Anthony, 1930–
Dead Wood
Poems 1953–83 Secker & Warburg 1984. © Anthony Thwaite
1984. Reproduced by permission of the author.

Tomlinson, Charles, 1927–
The Tree
Charles Tomlinson's Collected Poems Oxford University Press
1985. © Charles Tomlinson 1985. Reprinted by permission of the
author.

Vince, Michael, 1947–
The Memorial Trees
The Orchard Well Carcanet Press 1978. © Michael Vince 1978.

The Thicket
In the New District Carcanet Press 1982. © Michael Vince 1982.
Reprinted by permission of Carcanet Press.

Virgil, 70–19 BC
'Come, farmers, then, and learn the form of tendance'
from The Georgics Book II
Translated by L. P. Wilkinson, Penguin Classics 1982.
© L. P. Wilkinson 1982, reproduced by permission of Penguin UK.

Walcott, Derek, 1930–
  The Almond Trees
  The Gulf: Poems by Derek Walcott Farrar, Straus and Giroux
  1970. © 1970 by Derek Walcott. Reprinted by permission of
  Farrar, Straus and Giroux, LLC and Faber & Faber Ltd.

  'The oak inns creak in their joints as light declines'
  XXXVI *from* Midsummer
  Collected Poems 1948–84 Farrar, Straus & Giroux, New York
  1986. © 1986 by Derek Walcott. Reprinted by permission of
  Farrar, Straus and Giroux, LLC and Faber & Faber Ltd.

Watkins, Vernon, 1906–67
  Trees in a Town
  The Collected Poems of Vernon Watkins Golgonooza Press 1986.
  © Golgonooza Press 1986. Reproduced by permission of G. M.
  Watkins.

Whitman, Watt, 1819–1892
  'I Saw in Louisiana a Live-Oak Growing'
  'You Lingering Sparse Leaves of Me'
  The Complete Poems ed. Francis Murphy, Penguin 1975.

Wingfield, Sheila, 1906–1992
  Urgent
  Winter
  Collected Poems 1938–83 Enitharmon Press 1983. © Sheila
  Wingfield 1983. Reproduced by permission of Enitharmon Press
  and Hill & Wang, a division of Farrar, Straus and Giroux, LLC.

Wordsworth, William, 1777–1850
  'There is a thorn it looks so old' *from* The Thorn
  The Tables Turned
  Wordsworth & Coleridge Lyrical Ballads ed. H. Littledale, Oxford
  University Press 1959.

Young, Andrew, 1885–1971
  The Elm Beetle
  The Long-Tailed Tits
  The Tree
  The Tree-Trunks
  In Westerham Woods
  Selected Poems Carcanet Press 1998. © the Estate of the late
  Andrew Young 1960 & 1974. Reproduced by permission of
  Carcanet Press Ltd and The Andrew Young Estate.

Common Ground

Common Ground offers ideas, information and inspiration to help people to learn about, enjoy and take more responsibility for their own localities.

In the spectrum of environmental organizations Common Ground uniquely pioneers imaginative work on nature, culture and place. We link people, landscape, wild life, buildings, history and customs as well as bridging philosophy and practice, environment and the arts.

We explore new ways of looking at the world to excite people in to remembering the richness of everyday landscapes, common wild life and ordinary places, to savour the symbolisms with which we have endowed nature, to revalue our emotional engagement with places and all that they mean to us, and go on to become involved in their care.

In raising awareness and action through model projects, exhibitions, publications and events we are attempting to create a popular culture of wanting to care: we believe that the only way in which we shall achieve a sustainable relationship with nature is by everyone taking part in the effort. 'Holding Your Ground: an action guide to local conservation', 1985, established our role in informing local environmental action and cultural expression.

In reasserting the importance of liberating our subjective response to the world about us, we often work with people for whom this is everyday currency—poets, sculptors, composers, painters, writers, performers—people from all branches of the arts.

Our projects include: the campaign for Local Distinctiveness, Save our Orchards, Apple Day, Parish Maps, Local Flora Britannica, Rhynes, Rivers & Running Brooks and Confluence which is helping people to create new music for the River Stour in Dorset, Somerset and Wiltshire.

Common Ground is a charity (Charity No. 326335), formed in 1983. We seek no members and create no structures. Through collaborations we build links between organisations and disciplines, local people and professionals. We act as a catalyst and mentor; by broadcasting ideas and demonstrating by example we try to extend the constituencies of care for local nature and culture and create foundations for real democracy.

THE GREEN MAN · COMMON GROUND
TREES, WOODS &
IMAGE BY BEN NICHOLSON

Publications by Common Ground

Three anthologies of poetry have been edited by Angela King and Susan Clifford for Common Ground, published by Green Books in 2001, 2000 and 1998. Each brings together mainly 20th century poets with some older ones from both sides of the Atlantic in celebration of our relations with trees, rivers and fields in nature and in culture through the poetic imagination:

TREES BE COMPANY: foreword by John Fowles. (First published by Bristol Classical Press in 1989). 192 pages. £9.95 + £2.00 p&p.

THE RIVER'S VOICE: foreword by Roger Deakin. 224 pages. £9.95 plus £2.00 p&p.

FIELD DAYS: foreword by Adam Nicolson. 160 pages. £8.95 + £1.50 p&p.

A BOXED SET OF ALL THREE VOLUMES is also available, price £25.00 + £5.00 p&p.

THE COMMON GROUND BOOK OF ORCHARDS: *Conservation, Culture and Community,* published by Common Ground 2000. This book celebrates our best relations with nature. It explores how orchards continue to shape local culture and shows us many examples of how to value and celebrate traditional orchards, their delicate ecology and their local distinctiveness. It includes 50 photographs by James Ravilious and many more in colour and black and white. Large format 224 pages £18.95 + £5 p&p.

RIVERS, RHYNES AND RUNNING BROOKS: local distinctiveness and the water in our lives. A 48-page colour pamphlet. £4.00 including p&p.

LOCAL DISTINCTIVENESS: Place, Particularity and Identity, essays for a conference including papers by Neal Ascherson, Edward Chorlton, Sue Clifford, Gillian Darley, Roger Deakin, Michael Dower, Angela King, Richard Mabey and Patrick Wright. 1993. £5.95 + £1.50 p&p.

FROM PLACE TO PLACE: Maps and Parish Maps. Writings about maps and places. Sets the scene for an idea which challenges communities to explore, chart and care for the things they value in their everyday places. Writers including Barbara Bender, Robin Grove-White, Simon Lewty, Richard Mabey and Adam Nicolson are joined by people describing their experiences of Parish Mapping. 1996. £10.00 + £1.50 p&p.

For most recent information, please see our web site:
<www.commonground.org.uk>

Also available—two companion volumes:

THE RIVER'S VOICE

An Anthology of Poetry

Edited by Angela King and Susan Clifford

for Common Ground

With a Foreword by Roger Deakin

This volume comprises 190 poems by 133 poets: old favourites such as Tennyson's 'The Song of the Brook' and Wordworth's 'Upon Westminster Bridge' are joined by 20th century poetry from both sides of the Atlantic, with writers including A. R. Ammons, Wendell Berry, Carol Ann Duffy, U. A. Fanthorpe, Seamus Heaney, Ted Hughes, Andrew Motion, Sylvia Plath and William Carlos Williams.

UK edition published by Green Books
ISBN 1 870098 82 X £9.95

USA edition published by Chelsea Green
ISBN 1 890132 69 1 $16.95

FIELD DAYS

An Anthology of of Poetry

Edited by Angela King and Susan Clifford

for Common Ground

With a Foreword by Adam Nicolson

This anthology brings together the work of more than ninety poets, ancient and modern, including Wendell Berry, John Betjeman, John Burnside, Helen Dunmore, Ivor Gurney, Seamus Heaney, Elizabeth Jennings, John Keats, Alice Oswald, Kathleen Raine and Walt Whitman.

UK edition published by Green Books
ISBN 1 870098 73 0 £8.95

USA edition published by Chelsea Green
ISBN 1 890132 25 X $14.95